THE
SIMON PATCH
Story

Saga
of a
Rebel

Martha Dodge Wilkerson

ISBN: 1-4392-4312-3
ISBN-13: 9781439243121

Library of Congress Control Number: 2009905273

DEDICATION

To the memory of all those brave men and women who have ever served in the defense of this country and to all those who honor their memory.

L.K.D.

FORWARD

Simon Patch was born on a farm in Groton, Massachusetts, in 1749. His story, however, starts well before this—his pride and perseverance bred before he was given life—the desire to protect family and freedom running in the blood of his ancestors.

At the time of Simon Patch's birth, Groton was a well-established town that had been settled almost 100 years earlier. The town was no stranger to conflict and the fight for independence. Like many frontier towns, Groton residents fought long and hard against Native Peoples in the 17th century. The town was even abandoned for two years after a particularly vicious attack during King Philip's War in 1675 which left almost every building in the village burned to the ground. Settlers did return, and it is no surprise, then, that later generations of Groton men would go off to fight in subsequent battles and wars. As their forefathers had, men in Groton were insistent upon fighting for the future of their families and their town.

Simon's desire to push forward and prosper may have started with his decision to move to Ashby which was a small town situated some miles to the west of Groton. There, he could start his own farm, raise his own family and play a larger part in the development of the young town. His connections to Groton remained, however. It was here where most of his family resided, and it was here where he would ultimately be laid to rest.

Ashby sent men to fight the British some time after soldiers from Groton had already headed to battlefields. Their participation was just as valuable, of course. And Simon Patch followed the footsteps of many, including his brothers, who had embarked on this quest for freedom.

In the end, the towns now comprising the Nashoba Valley sent many men to various battles of the Revolution. Some of these soldiers never returned home to their families and others returned to live lives shortened by physical and emotional wounds received at war. Stones in the Old Burying Ground, ink on paper, and oral memories passed along, record the stories of those who were lost, those who came home, and all those who were affected. Simon Patch's story is one of these.

Concerning the authors of this book, the Dodge family has roots in Groton dating back to the 18th century. Leonard Dodge was born in Groton and lived in town for many years. Even after he relocated to New Hampshire, his assistance with town history was sought by local researchers. His wife, Fern Upton Dodge, a professional genealogist, did much of the research for this book. And, in the true spirit of continuing family traditions, their daughter, Martha Dodge Wilkerson, completed this story that her father started.

Kara E. Fossey
Groton Historical Society

CONTENTS

ACKNOWLEDGMENTS

This story would not have been possible without the dedication and professionalism of my wife, Fern Upton Dodge. In her quest for the facts she has contributed untold hours of research, providing along the way encouragement and suggestions as these characters came to life on the pages.

My thanks also to Ruth Bennett (deceased) of Groton, Massachusetts, who typed the first draft. Few would have been able to decipher my handwriting with such skill, and I owe her a debt of gratitude.

Many kind friends, some from distant places, have aided in this work. Without their interest, many facts presented here would not be available. I would like at this time to thank them all once again for their valued assistance.

Much time, patience and careful research has been expended on the military and medical aspects of this story. I have been aided in this effort by friends having access to military records, medical collections and medical libraries. Gaining information in the fields of hospitalization and military medicine of that day was a real challenge, and I was greatly aided by a friend who shared my enthusiasm. My heartfelt appreciation goes to Dr. Hugh G. Clark of Washington, D.C., whose research efforts and personal encouragement have made this endeavor possible.

L.K.D.

"The storm-winds urge the heavy weeks along,

Suns haste to set, that so remoter lights

Beckon the Wanderer to his Vaster home"

Ralph Waldo Emerson

PREFACE

In the northeast section of the Old Burying Ground in Groton, Massachusetts, a small American flag flies beside an old slate gravestone. The stone bears the following inscription:

(Cherub's Head)
Momento More
Here lies the
Body of Mr. Simon
Patch who was
wounded in ye de-
fence of his country
at ye white-plains
Octr 28th 1776 and
died of his wound
Decr 31st 1776 in ye
28th year of his age

This stone, as well as the stone marking the grave of his father on the right and his brother nearby, still stand erect and proud, silent monuments to the early defenders of an ideal. It is with pride and admiration that we Americans look back upon the accomplishments of these courageous people.

The newly purchased homestead upon which Simon Patch was at work when this story begins was in Ashby, Massachusetts, between Vinton Pond Road and New Townsend Road not far from Pearl Mill Brook. The deed describes it as containing fifty five acres with boundaries beginning at the Townsend-Lunenburgh town center. The forest long ago reclaimed this land, and the labor of man has been lost.

The homestead of Ebenezer Patch, father of Simon, in the easterly part of Groton consisted of a large new house nearing completion and later known as the "Gamlin Place." Still in excellent condition, this house and the great ash tree beside it stand as straight today as in the long ago when they sheltered the large Patch family and where scenes of drama and tragedy occurred. It is a reminder to thinking people of today of the strength of mind, body and purpose of that generation.

The house of Jacob, brother of Simon and one of the principals of this story, stood a half mile to the north. It is now gone, the victim of vandalism. In later years it was known as the John Henry Blood place.

The little old house of Isaac Patch, grandfather of Simon and father of Ebenezer, was a short distance west of the new house, its site marked by an old lilac bush. This house was probably torn down around 1800 by the Sawtell family who owned the property by descent as Simon's sister, Ruth, was married to Elnathan Sawtell on December 7, 1780.

The first of the Patch family in America was Nichols who appeared in Salem, Massachusetts, in 1636. Nicholas's son, John, born in England, married Elizabeth Brackenbury. Born in 1630, she is said to have been the first girl born in the Colony of Massachusetts Bay.

In reality this book began some years ago when the writer came into possession of some family papers, among them a letter written at Dartmouth College, Hanover, New Hampshire, on May 19, 1796. It was written by Jacob Patch, Jr. to his father in Groton. Jacob, Jr. was a medical student occupying room #4 on the first floor of the old dormitory. This interesting and descriptive letter relates details of the trip from Groton to Hanover by horse and sleigh and some details of life at Dartmouth. This letter would cause one to wonder if young Jacob's desire to become a doctor emerged from his knowledge of the horrific events through which his father and uncle passed during their participation in the Revolutionary War.

The basic facts of this story have been known to the writer for many years, and I have felt compelled to delve into the past. The interest this search aroused now brings you this true story. All local and military characters were real people, each one filling his proper place in the world of '75 and '76.

Local characters such as the families of Patch, Hazen, Wright, Chaplin, Prescott, Farwell, Farnsworth, Lawrence, Williams and many others were real residents of Groton at that time and are names which will be readily recognized by historians of that area. Each individual will be found doing his utmost to aid a cause in which he sincerely believed. All other characters are of course fictitious, the only exception being the tavern keepers who were real people running their respective taverns at that time. Quite naturally most conversation is imaginary; any exceptions to this are appropriately cited.

Weather conditions between October 28 and December 31, 1776, are entirely authentic as documented by Library of Congress records. The return journey from White Plains to Groton by litter is a fact. This painful and heartbreaking ordeal is illustrative of brotherly affection and Yankee determination, mingled with an undying love of home, family and country.

The route this journey follows was about the only one possible and that little better than a muddy trail. Roads in the interior of New England had not been encouraged by the English government, and this failure stimulated trade with the seacoast towns, benefiting English merchants. The condition of the route and the people and places along the way have been carefully studied and are, I believe, very typical. I believe that, more than 200 years after the events with which we are concerned, the facts presented are correct.

The events of the period covered by this story stimulated a desire to understand the personalities of the characters and how they withstood the events through which they passed. This became a compulsion, and the result is The Simon Patch Story: Saga of a Rebel, the story of the brief life, struggle and subsequent death of a young soldier during the American Revolutionary.

It is a story of dashed hopes and dreams and of the joy, sorrow, suffering and sacrifice of a typical colonial family.

1965
Leonard Kemp Dodge

PREFACE CONTINUED

More than forty years have passed since Leonard Dodge envisioned the completion of this narrative. It has been more than ten years since his death, leaving the work incomplete, but it was his legacy. As his only child I have felt a sense of duty and of honor in wishing to complete his mission, and so it is with great pride and appreciation that I dedicate my contribution to this story to my parents, Fern and Leonard Dodge. I hope the touches I have added will enhance their efforts in bringing this tale to you, the readers. Jacob Patch was my ggggggrandfather.

Martha Dodge Wilkerson

Chapter I

SIMON

Winter departed early in 1775. The warming ground was nearly free of stubborn frost although patches of slick ice and crystalline snow still lingered on the north sides of fences, and standing, murky water floated in muddy low spots. Each wispy current of air, so typical of that time of year, floated down and clutched handfuls of pearl-gray wood ashes, carrying them aloft only to release them to fall like fine, slightly soiled snow.

Simon, in the process of clearing another field of upland for hay and pasturage, on this day had been chopping brittle, gray limbs from fallen trees, piling brush and burning scrap. A glance at the smoke-shrouded sun told him that the day's work was about over. It was chore time. He was tired. He always felt fatigue after a long day in the field. His muscles ached, but it was a comfortable feeling. He knew his energy would be restored by morning, and he looked forward to the warmth of his home. In his mind's eye he could already smell the savory aroma that he anticipated would be coming from the kitchen hearth.

Ashby was home to Simon Patch and his family. Simon was one of those adventuresome few who dared risk adversity and unanticipated hardships to carve out a homestead in the new wilderness. Four years before this story begins he had purchased land, and in the summer of 1772 construction began on his modest house and barn. A native of Groton, Massachusetts, he unlike his brothers decided to strike out on his own in Ashby, only a few miles north and west of his parents' dwelling.

To some folks, perhaps ones from the city, Simon's primitive homestead would represent complete devastation, but to this young man, it smacked of progress. The larger, clean logs that he had felled were set aside to be hewed square for building or to be sawed into straight boards at the Ralph Hill Mill on Trap Falls Brook. Other, less desirable pieces were piled for use in the never-satisfied fireplace. Such was simple life on the frontier.

Simon Patch was the second son of Ebenezer and Sarah Patch. All of his siblings except for his older brother, Jacob, were younger and still living on the family homestead in Groton. Too many mouths for my father to feed, he had often thought when he was making the decision to strike out on his own with his new wife, Elizabeth. That farm cannot support us all. Some of us have to make it on our own.

Simon, only two years younger than Jacob, had always been the imaginative one, the dreamer, the visionary. He was dark-haired, tall and lean in contrast to his shorter, stockier, lighter complexioned sibling who was more pragmatic, serious and introspective. Neither brother could foretell the events that would soon unfold, binding them together in a way unimaginable and changing their lives forever.

Driving his ax into a stump, Simon straightened up and surveyed his surroundings. A wave of contentment enveloped him, that warm, cozy feeling one gets when one's life is going well, and he allowed his mind to wander. If only the now could last forever, he mused. If only I could stop the hands of our human clocks at this hour in this place forever so that nothing in our lives would change.

If only Elizabeth and the children would remain as they are on this particular glorious spring day. If only Papa and Mama would not get old. If only, if only. . .He had only to look around him at the changing seasons, at the dead and dying trees to recognize the impossibility of that thought. A flying bird on the wing brought him back to the task at hand.

He was glad that he did not use the clearing method of tree cutting then popular in Ashby. Under this system a section of forest was selected for destruction. Men worked during the winter sawing into each tree but not cutting it entirely through. Each tree was cut so that all trees would fall in the same direction. When the last few trees were cut off completely and simultaneously, they would press with the prevailing wind against those partially cut, and the whole forest would fall with one mighty crash. After drying for a year the entire mass would be set afire. It seemed so wasteful.

As Simon glanced out across the gently sloping field and beyond, he gazed upon land cleared in preceding years. Many rotting tree stumps still remained, but many had been removed earlier by ox team. Drawn into place, they provided temporary fencing. Later they would be replaced by carefully constructed stone walls, using rocks removed from the fields as part of the clearing process. Grass grew abundantly in the new fields, providing pasturage for his growing herd of cattle.

Simon turned and walked toward the house, remembering with the clarity of perfect hindsight that eventful day when everyone came together to raise the frame of the house and barn: the neighbors and cousin Stephen along with all the relatives from Groton and some from Westford, the in-laws, the Hazens and many members of the Blood and Lewis families.

At first there had been no floors, only loose boards laid in place, and a board resting across the timbers served as a shelf for dishes. A house without doors, windows or chimney. A temporary fireplace had been built outdoors for cooking. Fortunately a spring was not far from the house. In the autumn of that year the chimneys had been built, doors hung, windows placed, and the home was made more comfortable for the approaching winter.

Only twenty years earlier all the houses in Ashby had been constructed by placing hewn logs close together. Roofs had been built with timbers laid across the top upon which was placed dried bark, either birch or hemlock, in overlapping layers to protect from punishing rain and blistering snow. His house was so much better than those built earlier; he sighed contentedly.

Later on he knew it would be necessary to enlarge the existing frame and clapboard house as his family grew. The present building would become an ell to the elegant, classic house he would build that, he envisioned, would resemble his father's new house. In this new land, fertilized by the ashes of the forest, he would plant grain. Each year his crops would increase, and he would have plenty for his family and quite enough for the animals as well.

Dreams were forever cascading through Simon's mind; his hopes for the future, monumental. He had struck out on his own, and he wanted to make the most of every day and every opportunity. He had been only a child when his grandfather, Isaac Patch, died, but he remembered the many stories his grandfather had told him about what life was like in the old days, how difficult it had been, about coming to Groton to live in about 1727 and about serving as tythingman.

From those memories of his grandfather, Simon developed the desire to make a contribution to the development of Ashby as his grandfather had contributed to the development of Groton. He wanted to experience the sense of progress not only for himself but also for his family. More than anything, he wanted his sons to be proud of him. Why wouldn't it be possible, he speculated. Working alone as he often did provided ample opportunity to think and to dream. It was one of his favorite pastimes.

At the time Simon's house was erected, Ashby was only a fledgling town, although the number of inhabitants had increased steadily during the preceding few years. The town had been incorporated from parts of three neighboring towns, but its school districts were not laid out for another five years, and the town's meeting house was not considered complete for another six years. The town fathers had other concerns. There were bold and outspoken in their dislike of British rule, and in 1774 the town's stock of ammunition and arms had been replenished. When a crisis came, they would be prepared to lend to their neighbors in other towns.

There was no store in town; a store would not be built for another twenty years, but there were three innkeepers. Captain Samuel Stone in the east part of town owned an inn as did James Coleman in the west part of town. It is said that Jonas Bartlett also owned an inn. Stone's Tavern appeared to be the favorite stopping off place for travelers passing through. Ashby's first physician arrived last year, Dr. Thomas Carver. We are growing, albeit slowly, mused Simon, and I want to be part of it.

Simon, ax in hand, paused on the gentle knoll behind his house. He threw his shoulders back to relieve his aching muscles, and all weariness began to fall away. Pale sun streaked through the smoke-filled air, casting its late afternoon glow across the landscape. Scolding crows were suddenly silent.

A tiny bare spot of earth near the house appeared to take on that apple-green look reminiscent of spring. The door of his house opened, and his beautiful wife, Elizabeth, stepped out on the door rock followed by little Rebecca. Elizabeth also noticed that the lowering sun signaled day's end. What a fortunate young man he was. He felt blessed. A wave of warmth flooded over him.

Elizabeth waved her hand and then withdrew into the house. Perhaps little Simon, the third child, needed attention. Perhaps she left to stir the blazing fire and begin preparation of the simple evening meal that, as was the local custom, consisted of bread and milk for the children and women and bread, butter, cheese and cold vittles for the men.

Simon often referred to his wife as the "beautiful Elizabeth" but only to himself. His two younger brothers openly used this term to describe her, perhaps in admiration and perhaps in fun and surely as a compliment to one whom they both adored. As he walked toward the barn, his mind drifted back again on a situation that he had never spoken of to any one. The thought had never passed his lips and never would; he had promised himself that long ago.

Before he and Elizabeth were married, his older brother Jacob, then single, had courted her devotedly. She liked Jacob, and Jacob liked her, but for some still mystifying reason she had chosen to spend her life with Simon. Even now he was sometimes staggered and amazed by it all, and way down deep the unutterable, recurring thought periodically resurfaced that perhaps this mutual feeling between them was not yet ended.

Simon had never admitted to himself that this nagging thought perhaps had influenced him to accept the offer by his cousin, Stephen, to purchase half of the land Stephen had purchased earlier of the well-known Abijah Willard. Maybe Stephen had sensed this situation himself and was thereby prompted to make the offer.

Come now, Simon Patch, be yourself. You know this line of thinking is ridiculous. Forget it. Wasn't Elizabeth right there in your house preparing your supper? What more do you want? Life is certainly good, isn't it? Spring is all but here, the future looks wonderful. Could any young man in this year of 1775 ask for more?

Chapter II

AN EARLY SPRING EVENING

Simon wearily leaned his hand-worn ax handle against the grind-stone by the barn door as a reminder to sharpen the much-used blade early in the morning. He methodically tended his livestock, wanting to finish before darkness descended. The daylight hours were still short, but then again, the days were never long enough to do everything he wanted. The seven geese were virtually carefree. An equal number of sheep needed little more attention. Two cows needed to be milked and, along with the horse and pair of oxen, needed hay and water sufficient until morning.

To finish the evening ritual Simon drew gelid water from the well and brought it, along with a still warm bucket of fresh, sweet milk, to the kitchen. Later from the pile by the sheltered end of the house he would bring wood for the evening fire as well as for the next morning.

The setting sun in a sky embellished with golden splendor fore-told of another magnificent day to follow, and the great blue dome above began to shed a lucent light as stars appeared in sudden and increasing numbers to commence their nightly vigil. Warmth of day was replaced by the still, crisp chill of an early spring evening.

Evening was the favorite time of day for this family. Simon was away from the house from early morning until near dusk so it was only at this time that he was able to enjoy his children, Rebecca nearing her fifth birthday, Nathan just past four and little Simon who would be one year old in a few days.

A blast of warm air greeted him as he leaned against the kitchen door. Elizabeth rushed to meet him, relieving him of the pail of milk. "Here, le' me take that. Hungry tonight, love? You've cut up many trees today, I see. Now, you children do as I say and stand back from the fire or you'll get burned."

Simon replied that, yes, he was starving as he scooped up all three children into his arms at once. "Papa, Papa," they all shouted in unison, "Come play with us!" He proceeded to entertain them while Elizabeth completed preparation of their simple supper.

The compact, inviting kitchen was dominated by a huge fireplace, covering nearly the entire west wall of the room. A recently stoked fire burned hot-orange as Simon slumped into a straightbacked chair with all of his children clinging to him, tugging his hair and pulling at his shirt, not wanting to release their grasps for even a moment.

A bit of roughhousing was another ritual in which he joyfully indulged as Elizabeth worked, while he savored the familiar smells of the day's cooking, the residual aroma of bread baked early in the morning and meat that had been roasting all day. As the fire began to die down, it threw off a burnt russet glow that reached the far corners of the room.

Elizabeth was proud of how well they had managed to furnish their new home. Some house wares were gifts from her family, the Williams', and her mother's family, the Nuttings, and from Simon's extended family and friends. She particularly cherished her complete set of pewter plates, platters, spoons, pots, porringers and basins. These were a gift from Simon even before they had moved to Ashby. She felt only a few things were lacking.

Evenings were usually spent in some productive enterprise. Elizabeth often knit or spun. She was skillful with either the great or little wheel. Simon often whittled out of wood a tool handle or perhaps made a wooden tying yoke for a calf. Some evenings he read as he possessed a larger number of books than most young men. Many evenings Stephen came to visit and often ate supper with them. Stephen, as yet unmarried, had been too busy to marry but was planning to when he had his place in good condition. This night Elizabeth showed no inclination to either knit or spin but sat down by the fire, "Simon, I think I know what you've been thinking about lately." Her silky, chestnut brown hair danced with golden highlights from the fireplace, and Simon thought that she had never looked lovelier.

"Probably so", he replied with a grin. "It would be easy to guess. You know I have thought all winter about only one subject, our future."

"Now I have your problem on my mind too now that spring's 'bout here," Elizabeth absentmindedly commented, kicking a coal as it sparked out onto the hearth. "I've been so sad all winter because of father's death last December and I'm frettin' about the changes it may make in the family. I know that I can't help them none. I'm as much use to them as two thumbs! So I've decided to worry about us for a change. I have been thinking about what you said 'bout wantin' to be a trader!"

"So have I! Heavens to Betsey, Elizabeth! I know lots of reasons why it's a good venture," chuckled Simon, thinking Elizabeth ill-informed, "Let's go over it again, and then you can tell me why you don't think it's such a good idea." Indulgently, "First, an opportunity exists. Almost everyone I ever heard of who became a trader made himself a lot of money, and that's something we need badly. It's much more profitable than farming, but I'll always love the farm best." Simon paused, reaching over to touch Elizabeth's hand with his forefinger, communicating without words his wish that she hear him out. "Now don't say it! I know father has prospered mightily, but much of his success has been good luck in acquiring land favorably, and he had four boys who helped him out a lot." Elizabeth sighed in resignation, knowing his point of view was entirely valid.

"Now just think how this Bay Colony is growing," he continued. "These towns are filling up with new people. Take Ashby for example, in 1750 hardly anyone was living here. It was incorporated not ten years ago. There were forty three families here then, but there was no government. So, as you remember, the incorporators asked James Prescott from Groton to call and conduct the first meeting.

Simon took a deep breath, "Six years ago there was no meeting house. Now it is built and furnished all but those few gallery pews. Two years ago the school districts were laid out. Ralph Hill has a saw mill. William Hobart has a grist mill over the hill by the Townsend line. There are three people who have inn-holder's licenses. Last year Doctor Carver came to town. But no one has opened a store!

Simon continued softly, "A store and trading with teams traveling to Boston and back somehow all belong together as you can readily understand. I must admit that right now while the port in Boston is closed, times are bad. Some day, somehow, of course, the port will be reopened.

"Think of all the things we have in the country that those poor people in Boston need," he continued, "When the day comes when the port is open again, there will be hardly any limit to the business that a man could do. Think of all the things that must be hauled to Boston: meat, firewood, potatoes, wool, hay, grain, hides, charcoal, boards, lath, shingles, clapboards, apples and cider. Now when the teams come back they could bring salt, cloth, glass, paper, lots of iron things, pewter and books. Until last fall when the Continental Congress stopped importation, there were goods such as molasses, syrups, coffee, tea, wines, indigo, and this is but part of the list. Speaking of wood, our fire is dying out. I'll throw another log on."

On January 3, 1775, Groton's town clerk, Oliver Prescott, had recorded that it had been voted to accept the recommendation of the Continental Congress to prohibit the purchase or sale of any good from England or Ireland, molasses, syrups, panela, coffee or pimento from the British plantations or Domingo, wines from Madeira or the Western Islands or foreign indigo.

"Now is the time to get started," he suggested, "When this period of uncertainty is over, there will be a great rush of business. Other men will get this same idea. Just imagine a store down in the center of town such as Mr. Cutler has in Groton and a number of teams on the road. Just think of it! The farmers all around here, bringing goods to the store to trade for goods from Boston. Those things and many more picked up along the way to sell in the city. It's the biggest thing there is.

"People along the road through Townsend will have goods to sell. The Symonds and Lakins and Kemps up on the Throne. Remember all the pasture land that the Lakins have and that big field near Flat Pond. Why, there are sixty acres in that one field! They could raise even more cattle than they do now. Down by the river there is the big Blood farm and on the other side more Bloods, Jenkins, Farnsworths, and Greens, even before you get to the center of Groton. Father and Jacob and your folks and lots more will have goods to sell. They don't want to have to go to the city, and they don't have the time. They also have to buy things that I could bring back." Simon was speaking rapidly now, his eyes bright with excitement.

Elizabeth looking up from the fire and speaking quickly so as not to appear to interrupt quietly countered, "Uh, hu, all you say is true, and it makes good sense. I don't know anything about business, but I do know that what you want to do would take a lot of money that we don't have! You are young and brave with lots of gumption, Simon, and I love these things about you, but I'm scared to see you take on so much. Where will the money come from? Do you know?"

"Well, no, not right offhand, " admitted Simon.

"You said you could have several teams on the road at once. Cattle and carts and such cost money. If you raised the animals yourself, even if they didn't cost much in food, would take years. Then you'd have to train 'em," her voice trailed off. "All that would slow your start. Here's another thing, a store building large enough for all you want to do would cost a fortune. Oh, Simon, you will think badly of me for talking this way, but we got to think of all sides of the question."

"You are right, of course, Elizabeth, but I am sure I can hire the money somewhere for such a fine opportunity. There is Mr. Willard, for one."

"No," said Elizabeth sharply.

"Well, then, I could—"

Elizabeth seldom interrupted Simon, but tonight was different. "Have you thought about all the men you would have to have? Where would you find them?"

"As sure as there are stars in the heavens, that, my dear, is the easiest of all," replied Simon, smiling. "You have five brothers. Four of them are grown men. Surely they are not needed on the farm, that is, all the time. One of my brothers could be away some of the time. Then there is the Hazen family with three grown boys. Their farm is small, and they work out some. I am sure they would work for me. Now I have not gone out of the family to name all these. Every one I have mentioned, you must admit, is fully trust-worthy, and I am sure each of them would be glad to be away from home at least part of the time. There is a certain appeal about the unknown and the possibility of adventure in traveling, you know."

"No, I don't know", retorted Elizabeth with tears welling up in her eyes, "but I'm sure of this! It'd be dangerous. Runaways, accidents, bad weather. Highway men on the roads! Remember the stories about that old man King and his renegades? There're thieves and cutthroats in Boston. I'm beginning to worry already. Oh, I'm so sorry, Simon."

"Well, " said Simon after a slight pause while he pondered how to deal with his wife's bewilderment, "I guess I won't have to worry about your worries, Elizabeth. Come out of it now, my dear. We both know it would work out all right. You know all the men I have mentioned. Half of them are your own brothers. Don't you think that every one of them can take care of himself anywhere? You never see me cross one of my brothers-in-law, do you?"

Elizabeth brightened at Simon's jest as he hoped she would, and he changed the subject, "Do you realize that two drivers can handle three teams when traveling together? The handiest team you place in the middle without a driver, and by keeping the teams close together they soon learn to follow the lead team. The first and last teams of course have drivers. I've seen it done often."

"Simon, you've always been one to take chances, and I love you for it," responded Elizabeth pausing, "Jacob would never take a risk like that. Oh, my, how can anybody plan for anything when our colony is in such turmoil. Who have you talked with about this? What does your father say? He'll know as well as any other body what you should do. It would never do to ask Mr. Cutler or Mr. Lewis. Let's try and think of someone here in Ashby who knows something 'bout bein' a trader. Or, why don't you go down and ask James Prescott. He's a man people look up to."

"I had thought of talking with him," said Simon.

"And another thing. What if fighting and rioting start in Boston? Folks say it could happen. I 'spect we don't hear all that goes on out there. There may be a real war with all those horrible English and Hessian soldiers, and our people so mad! That Mr. Adams and rich Mr. Hancock making speeches. Simon, Mr. Hancock is a merchant and very rich, too, I hear. But no, forget about that. When towns like Groton and Ashby are forming their own Minutemen companies what can you do but wait and see? Stephen has joined."

Simon sighed and was about to speak, when Elizabeth said, "Well, let's wait until morning anyway".

Chapter III

EBENEZER'S PROMISE

Down in Groton a stocky, brown-haired youth whose usual placid demeanor has been replaced by a determined and worried look, strode purposefully between two muddy ruts in the path known as "Dunstable Road". It was early evening in the spring and still dark for the hour.

A wane sun had plunged beneath the tree line, leaving the air damp and chilly but with promise of seasonal newness ahead. As he walked, Jacob Patch reflected on his young family, Mary (Hazen) his wife, and on the antics of little Jacob and baby Sarah. He did not like leaving them alone in the evening, but he had been summoned.

Ahead on the left loomed the bulk of his father's new house and out buildings silhouetted against the faint salmon-colored light of the western sky. Glad they are living in that house, he thought, even if there are a few things yet to be done, some finish and other details. The blockade of Boston harbor prevented the procurement of nails, so any building would have to be postponed.

Turning into the yard, still muddy from snow melt, he walked around the corner to the west door of the kitchen and gently pushed it open. The comfort of this familiar scene would become fixed in his mind and later recalled in times of stark loneliness and bitter despair.

The kitchen fireplace midway of the long room was on his left. In it smoldered a bed of coals. Immediately beyond, the steep, narrow, winding back stairs rose sharply to a bedroom above where the youngest children slept. Flashing through Jacob's mind was the long family debate on the location of these stairs that was finally settled by Sarah in her maternal wisdom. Beneath the stairs were those leading to the great dirt floor cellar below, his father's triumph, nine feet deep and full size of the house. Nothing would ever freeze down there, Ebenezer had said. Further yet was the door to the west front room.

Jacob's younger sister, Ruth, was puttering about with the last of the evening chores. Beyond the shelf where she was stacking plates was the south door of the kitchen, and just outside were the newly dug well and finely-fashioned well sweep.

Two newly placed fresh logs were beginning to burn brightly, shedding a bright red and yellow light all over. Facing the fire but with backs to him sat his two younger brothers, Benjamin and Oliver. Also facing the fire in his favorite well-worn chair sat his father, Ebenezer, exposing to Jacob the profile of this usually placid, always intelligent face, but that now bore a strangely strained and contorted look. At that moment the dancing shadows from the fire emphasized every line of that familiar face, and for the very first time Jacob thought his father looked old and tired.

"I tell you boys, something is about to break open." Catching sight of Jacob from the corner of his eye, "Oh, Jacob, it's good that you have come. We're expecting you, and I waited so I could tell all of you the news. Get a chair and sit here with me." As he was instructed, Jacob brought a ladder back chair from the side of the room closer to the fire, nodded to his brothers and placed his hand affectionately on Ebenezer's shoulder.

"Well, y' know that I went to town this afternoon and I almost wished that I had stayed here and worked with you lads and not heard the things I listened to in town. After all the trouble in Boston and the folks up in Portsmouth takin' over the fort and haulin' away the powder this winter, I thought trouble was on all sides of us. Then last month all you young fellows got together and organized the two Minutemen companies and now violence right in our own town. It's awful, I tell you–."

Sarah coming down the back stairs from tucking in the children voiced everyone's collective thoughts, "For land's sake, Ebenezer, control yourself and hurry up and tell us what's happened."

"Well", said Ebenezer taking a deep breath and tipping his chair back so that it rested only on its two back legs, "When I got to the top of the hill just back of the church I could see a crowd of people around Mr. Cutler's store, so I stopped there first. You will remember what a terrible windy day Sunday was, so bad we didn't go to church. Well, it was much worse up there on the hill, and it blew down the horse sheds there by the church."

"My foot, Father, is that what I came way down here to hear about?" exclaimed Jacob, impatiently and uncharacteristically springing from his chair.

"Oh, sit down, Jacob, please," proclaimed Ebenezer dismissively. "I have scarce begun. I'll tell you about Reverend Dana's sermon first. I can't tell you exactly what he said, for everyone I talked with told it different, but he definitely lined himself up with the King and Parliament and came right out and said that we here in the Bay Colony were wrong in opposing all the taxes and laws that Parliament has burdened us with! Now what do you think of that?"

"Land sakes!" exclaimed Sarah.

"Not surprised," proffered Benjamin.

"People pretty upset?" inquired Oliver.

"Upset! Why, after church folks stayed and talked the whole thing over and decided to hold a special meeting the next day. That was yesterday. Well, they had the meeting and as near as I can tell nothing was done except everyone had a chance to have his say. And just listen to this: Just about dark after the meeting someone went out back of the store and fired a musket at Mr. Dana's house! Why, you can see the bullet hole and the splintered clapboard between the two upper windows clear from the road!"

"Well, great blushing tom cats! Things are jumpin'," exclaimed Jacob, "What's next?"

"Lots of people think the Reverend should not be allowed in church next Sunday," Ebenezer continued.

Ruthie, wiping off the kitchen table for the fifth time, said quietly, "Just think, in our own town and in our own church, too!"

Ebenezer continued, "The store was filled with people, all talking at the same time. No business, just talk. Mr. Cutler just not saying anything to anyone, just taking it all in, he was. The yard out front was full of small groups of people; everyone was a'talkin and looking toward Mr. Dana's house. The census taken ten years ago counted over 1,400 people in town, and it seems as if most of them were in the village this afternoon!"

"Isn't it a matter for the selectmen," suggested Jacob, "They are in charge of town affairs."

"But, Jacob, this is a church matter," sighed Sarah her face sadly showing that a dark cloud had settled over her much beloved church.

"Well, I kind of think so, too, Jacob," agreed Ebenezer. "The selectmen should call a meeting. I don't believe Mr. Dana ever will."

"What the town needs," spoke up Oliver, "is a preacher like the Reverend Mr. Webster from Temple, You all heard him preach last month when the companies invited him here. We knew then that Dana was against us. That's why we wanted no more of him."

"I haven't told it all yet, boys," continued Ebenezer. " I went down the road to Jonathan Clark Lewis's trading store; he wants me to bring in some supplies next trip. They were all excited there about the Association paper. You remember the covenant that Congress asked all the towns to support? We all signed on to it a while back, January, I think. The selectmen say that everyone in town has signed except four men, and they will be given one more chance to do so."

"Tar and feathers," muttered Benjamin, striking a clenched fist against his open palm.

"The selectmen won't tell yet who the four are," Ebenezer continued. "Well, after listening to all the threats that have been made and talking to a couple of travelers who stopped in, I had had enough so I started home without doing any of my errands. Being down in the village I thought I had better come home by way of the Row, and I stopped at Jason Williams place for a few minutes."

"Have they seen Simon and Elizabeth lately?" interrupted Sarah.

"No," replied Ebenezer, "but I think they're going up in a few days. He is just as upset as I am. Jason says the boys are all worked up and are talking about war breaking out any time. He says they all say they will go when the time comes. Perhaps they are right; I don't know. I came home the long way by Skull Hole and up over the hill instead of by Blood's. Riding along I got to thinking of all the things that have happened over the last few years." Ebenezer dropped his chair back to the floor again and leaned forward, resting one hand on his knee and prodding a log on the fire with the other. The crackling flames restored warmth to the room.

"You just listen up," he continued, "The Stamp Act, it was in the spring about ten years ago. The tea was thrown in Boston harbor a year ago last December. In March of last year the King closed the port at Boston. A year ago this spring the regulars marched from Boston to Marblehead looking for powder, but our boys turned 'em back. About the same time the Britishers tarred and feathered that poor man from Billerica. A couple of years ago at a town meeting everyone agreed not to buy any more tea. I guess I mentioned that affair at Portsmouth last winter. The Grievance Committee reported a list of grievances concerning our rights and liberty."

"Hold on a minute, father," interrupted Jacob, "You talked with a lot of people today. Did any one except the Williamses think that all these things mean war now?"

"Oh, yes," Ebenezer hastened to add. "I would say that more than half, probably three-quarters of the people said so in one way or another."

Benjamin had been listening silently while thoughtfully watching the fire slowly change the two red oak logs to glowing coals. He suddenly struck his knees with his open palms and half rising from his chair exclaimed in a low voice, "I'll bet I know who fired that shot! I remember something someone said one of the last times I was up town."

This brought an immediate and unusually sharp response from Ebenezer. "Ben, if you even have an idea on the subject you will keep it strictly to yourself!"

"Yes, sir," said Benjamin.

The silence that followed was broken by Oliver who said, "I think we had best plan what we should do."

Jacob quickly concurred, "Yes, so do I if so many people think that trouble is at hand. Father, what do you think we need to do now?"

The fireplace coals cooled, but no one stepped forward to re-invigorate the flames with another log. Sarah and Ruth sat silently in the background, each deep in her own thoughts. Not one of the boys wanted to break the mood of the moment. The air was kinetic yet somber.

Ebenezer hesitated for only a moment, speaking with measured intent, "Boys, this is how I feel. If trouble comes, some or all of us will be called away to serve where we can. This, we as a family can do nothing about, nor would we; nor can we change it. Those of us who may be left here at home will have a very heavy responsibility to look after the women folk and the children. This farm and Jacob's can easily care for all of us and more. Just think, it can give us shelter, and should this house be destroyed for any reason, there is plenty of timber at hand to rebuild it.

"The farm can provide animals for power as well as meat. There will be grain, vegetables and fruits in abundance for all of us and plenty of them! The farm can provide fuel and clothing. Beyond these things we need little else. I need not remind you, however, that to produce these things we must work long and hard. We have always done so, but in this difficult time we must think to aid our neighbors and to provide for the men who will be fighting the battles.

"This is a large house, and we still have my father's old house too so we have plenty of room for, well, your family, Jacob, and Mary's folks too if need be. If Simon's family or Stephen's, for that matter, need a house, we can provide it.

"In fact this house will be open to all loyal Americans of good will. We must all work very hard, but I am sure that justice will prevail. Some day we will enjoy the prosperity and freedom that will be ours when these dark days have past. Remember, Providence will provide for those who have faith. That is what I believe, boys."

The sky was black as ebony by the time Jacob left to return home. Lit only by a few stars above, it was a lonely, slow walk down Dunstable Road, the silence of the night broken only by his footfalls.

Chapter IV

OUR WORLD

Ebenezer Patch's two youngest sons stood in the doorway of the barn waiting for their father as he approached from the house. "Well, boys," said Ebenezer, "I think we had best go back down to the woods with the team and keep on hauling out the wood for the charcoal burn. Your mother wants us to take grain to the mill today, too, so perhaps. . ."

A shrill, earsplitting scream and the resonating bang of a hastily slammed door were heard across the bridle path. Ruthie, the oldest girl of the family now twelve years old, came running to them, "Papa, papa! Mother says I can go to the mill. I want to go. You know how I love to go down there, and Mother prefers Mr. Prescott's grist to Mr. Gilson's. She said she thought Mr. Gilson's millstones needed fixing. And Papa, isn't it Oliver's turn to go? It's only fair for the boys to take turns isn't it, Papa? Say we can go, Papa, ple-e-ase."

Ebenezer's look of harried annoyance vanished, and he turned a broad smile upon his much loved daughter, "Yes, Ruthie, we will have it any way you want it. You have been a great help to your mother. Oliver, go get the horse ready. I think I had best send along some of Jacob's corn too. I'm sure he still has some stored in our crib. Don't take too much. Before long, warm weather will be with us again, and that ground grain won't keep very long when it's hot. Ruthie, what about Ede and Sammy, do they want to go along? Go and ask! It is getting late. Everyone get going now."

A few minutes later Ruthie was back impatiently waiting for her brother to finish harnessing the horse and loading the grain onto the wagon. The wagon was simple but functional. Consisting of a flat bed, it was sufficiently long to haul goods to town and could be pulled by a single horse.

"Hurry, Oliver," Ruthie admonished, "We won't have to wait for Sammy. Mother says he hasn't brought in wood for the day so he can't go. Ede doesn't want to go either. The only place she wants to go is to town where she can stare at strange people she has never seen before and stand in front of Mr. Quarles' bake shop and smell the gingerbread baking." The bakery sign read "Gingerbread, Cake and Bisket Sold Here", but it was only the gingerbread that Ede loved.

Oliver smiled, nodding in agreement, "I've noticed she never misses a trip to town."

At last they were off. Wagon wheels crunched on muddy ruts that had dried into crispy ridges. "Which way do you want to go, Ruthie?"

"Let's go the back road and come home the upper road." Oliver deftly guided the horse and its load out onto the road. "Oliver, let's play a game! We can pretend that you have never been on this trip before. You can be a cousin from some way-off place, Boston, perhaps, and I will tell you about all the things we see just as Father told them to me."

"That's fine," Oliver responded absentmindedly not yet ready to join in this happy pastime of his sister, "And see that you don't miss a thing. What do we do here at this turn of the road?"

"Oh, yes! I almost forgot. Turn left here," said Ruth still too excited to be thinking clearly. "Right around this short curve in the wall. What an interesting job Grandpa did on that wall." Ruthie stretched her arms out as though to embrace the entire world.

"What a wonderful morning to go for a ride. Just look, these great tall trees on both sides of us all the way down the hill. Their leaves aren't all the way out yet, but they will be soon. Then the foliage will be too thick to see through. I hope Father never cuts them down."

"Probably he won't. The land right there is too steep to plow," commented Oliver, guardedly. He was having a hard time getting used to being a cousin from Boston.

Ruth shivered slightly in the spring air. Even though the leaves were little more than buds, the branches were sufficiently full and dense on the massive old trees to provide a chilly cover. April in Massachusetts is unpredictable. Cool days interspersed with others of surprising warmth conspire to bring forth the burst of May blooms. Days full of sunshine alternate with torrential rains, washing away residual snows and patches of ice, filling streams to their brims and spilling them into the surrounding fields. The sun begins to warm the earth, tempting creatures and humans alike to stretch their limbs and renew their love affair with their environment.

"Now we are coming to Cow Pond Brook, and don't ask me why it's called that. I can't find out. I guess no one else knows either," Ruth mused, "Do you suppose the water is too deep for the horse to wade through? He'll likely decide that for himself after he stops for a drink, don't you think?"

"Whose little house is that on the right on the other side of the brook?" queried Oliver, trying to keep Ruthie engaged in her game.

The horse, his thirst satisfied, struggled for secure footing in the deep, dark water of the racing brook and carefully pulled his load out of the water and up the slippery slope to safety. Muddy water dripped from the wheels of the wagon as it lurched back onto the road. With a sigh of relief Ruth continued her story, "This is Mr. William Parker's house. I don't see anyone around." Ruthie's eyes darted in all directions, looking for any signs of life. "Oh, I almost forgot to tell you, on our left but out of sight below this ridge is Hunting Swamp. It is about opposite this road to the right. That is called Nutting's Road, I guess because the Nutting family lives out there. It goes over near Millstone Hill, I think."

"I see," said Oliver. "Tell me about this field on the left."

"Oh, it's a lovely field," Ruth said gazing contentedly at the still dried ochre grass, "and I call it the daisy field. You should be here later on in the summer, and you'll see what I mean."

"Maybe I'll still be around then," replied her brother woefully. Oliver recalled with great mental clarity that particular field. The first hay would be cut in June, and by August the field would be covered with a rainbow of colors, white and yellow daisies and Queen Anne's lace intermingled with the reddish-purple of Indian paint brush and the white and lavender of clover. A regular feast for the eyes, Oliver recalled, and food for the soul.

"And now we come to the mill pond. This is our brook again, and the water held in this pond runs Mr. Tyng's saw mill which is just around this corner. My, just smell the pine. I love fresh pine sawdust. Let's stop for a few minutes and watch the saw go up and down and see the water pour over the wheel."

Ruthie's reference to the smell of pine evoked for Oliver memories of years past and walks in the woods at this very time of year when plant life is waking up from its winter sleep. The only sound to break the silence would be the crunch of his shoes as they broke tiny filaments of dried debris. He recalled the mustiness of spring time. And as the seasons changed to summer, the smell changed to a sweetness that refreshed the nostrils as one walked through deep beds of pine needles and moss. Not at all like the smell of sawdust, he recalled.

Nearly mesmerized, they watched water flow over the mill wheel like white and blue fluid icicles that changed form again and again as they dropped from one paddle of the wheel to the next. Water gurgled and churned competing with the whine of the wheel itself, a harmony of sights and sounds. After a few minutes Oliver clucked to the horse, raising the reins in a signal to move on. They were on their way again with Ruth pointing out the small sulfur spring in the woods to the right, and then they crossed the brook that ran into the Great Massapoag a few rods west of the road.

"This land along here on the east side of the road," Ruth recalled, "belongs to the Sewall family, and the little brook up ahead is called Sewall's Brook. The land along the shore of the pond belongs to the Tyngs, and Grandpa used to say that old Mr. Tyng bought it from an Indian named Peter Jethro and that it was a turf and twig deed."

Although he already knew the answer to this question Oliver asked, "What in the world is a turf and twig deed, Ruthie?" Ruth, pleased to have been asked, proudly explained the very ancient ceremony of transferring land when, in the presence of witnesses, the seller digs a handful of turf, breaks a twig from a tree and sticking the twig in the bit of sod, passes it to the purchaser.

"This land north of the brook and on up past the Gulf was sold by two Indians to Mr. Edward Cowell who was a rich man, a merchant in Boston. Papa said the Indians were Kanepatund and Patatnick."

"Well, this is all very interesting," offered Oliver gravely, hoping to appear entirely ignorant of the local traditions so proudly repeated by his younger sister. "Who lives in that house over to the right whose roof we see from here?"

"That's the Blodgett place," replied Ruth. "Take this road to the left, and we'll soon be at the mill."

The mill and mill house were at that time owned by Jonas Prescott, Jr. While waiting their turn and watching the slowly turning millstones reduce whole grain to the desired fineness, Ruthie plied the miller with questions and soon had him explaining to them his version of the flood that had destroyed the natural embankment and sealed the Gulf, creating this ideal mill site for the first mill owned by Mr. Samuel Adams. He pointed to several places on the ridge on the other side of the ford way that still plainly showed the old waterline, many feet above the present level of the pond. Astounding, thought Oliver. It looks as though the area has always looked as it does right now. It's hard to imagine it looking differently.

Ruth kept the miller talking until another team arrived bringing grist. Even Oliver did not hurry as he was enjoying the tranquil scene, the sleek shining pond stretching off far to the south, the heavily wooded, steep ridges rising high on both sides of the spring-swollen brook, the old mill and the small nearby dwelling house at the foot of the high ridge on the west side of the brook, close to the now almost impassable ford way. He was glad he had come along on this little excursion. He was even enjoying Ruthie's game. It has a break from the daily routine of farm life.

As they left this very special place, Ruth suggested that they follow what had been the first road between Groton and Dunstable known as the "Groton Path." Grandfather Patch had said that the old folks told him it followed an Indian trail from the Merrimac River to Wachusett Mountain. Now this old road seemed to be just another wood road until it joined the new road to Groton out beyond where Mr. Spaulding lived.

The road turns left away from a meager pond formed by the work of diligent beavers who had created a dam. After crossing what Ruthie said was Green's Brook, they came out on the "upper road" along the ridge where to their left sunshine sparkled on a pristine lake in the distance that could be seen through an occasional break in the endless phthalo pine forest. To Ruthie's delight, Oliver pretended total ignorance when she pointed out that the narrow road on the right led to Jacob's Tub Meadow and to Tub Meadow Brook.

"Oliver! Do you know what I think?" she asked rhetorically, "I think this is the best trip in the world for people who will just take the time to appreciate what they are looking at. I hope I can live right here always. Say I can, Oliver," pleaded Ruthie, "It frightens me when I hear all of you and father talk about the horrible things going on in Boston. . . It is a nice trip up to Simon's, too. Next time we go up there let's get Father to tell us about what we are seeing after we cross the river and up over the Throne." The Throne was a hill 484 feet high in the western part of town near the Townsend line on the top of which was a level field of sixty acres containing a small pond.

"Fine," said Oliver laughingly, "We'll do it! By the way, I recognize the road to the right; doesn't that lead right to Jacob's house?"

"That's right. We're almost home. Oliver! Let's stop pretending for a minute. I want to ask you a question. Why did grandfather build this—well I would call it a double jog in this wall right here? There's no big rock or anything else in the way."

"I've wondered the same thing," replied Oliver. "It must be twenty feet out from a straight line and then back again. I asked Father once, and he said Grandfather just laughed about it. I think he did it just to make people wonder and ask questions, or maybe he just needed a place to put all the rocks! His own private joke, I would say."

I'll bet that was it," agreed Ruth. "Oliver! Pretending is on again. This nice, big, new house up ahead belongs to Ebenezer Patch, and that is where I live with all my wonderful family. If everything could go on just as it is now, wouldn't it be just perfect? When everything is fine and the world around us is so peaceful, how could we wish for anything more? But Oliver, somehow I am afraid. I don't know what it is, but something frightens me." Ruthie's now husky voice trailed off. Oliver had no response.

Chapter V

A Call To Arms

It was Wednesday. Westward and across the road from Ebenezer's house was an orchard and its adjunct, the family cider mill. Recently pruned, thrifty, thinly branched apple trees covered the sloping east side of the hill. Each spring after the snows mysteriously vanished, branches broken by winter storms had to be cleared away along with unwanted undergrowth that would make the foliage too thick if left unmanaged.

Soon swelling buds will usher in a mass of pinkish white blossoms, covering each tree like a delicate veil. The fragrant aroma of each blossom will then fan out; and when a breeze toward the west arises, perfume from each blossom will converge, descending on the house like a blanket covering a bed. Urgency was called for as the orchard clean-up must be completed before the blossoms arrive to avoid accidental injury to any low-hanging branches. Ebenezer always insisted on doing the orchard work himself while Benjamin and Jacob took on the other spring chore, fence mending.

It was barely sun up. Ebenezer had been working only about an hour or two when he suddenly became aware of hoof beats way off in the distance. Knowing that his boys were not using the horses, his curiosity was aroused. He stopped to listen, and he was alarmed to hear shouts that seemed to come from the direction of the house.

The peace and tranquility of the homestead was being rudely disrupted. As he listened, he heard childish voices and then receding hoof beats rapidly fading away. Perhaps a fire or an accident in the neighborhood, he thought, but this rider did not turn back after summoning aid. The idea of neighborhood tragedy was immediately replaced by an even more alarming one. These times were not normal; anything could happen. Could it be that the fateful day of reckoning had arrived?

Ebenezer listened for more clues before turning toward the house but broke into a run when he heard panic in Ruth's voice, "Papa, Papa, where are you? Where are the boys. The man said to call the boys."

"God's green footstool! What did he want? Who was it?" called Ebenezer as he caught sight of Ruthie. He could feel his heart beating in his chest; he could even hear it. Sweat broke out on his face; his mind was racing.

Ruth, obviously frightened, her voice somewhat tremulous, "I don't know who he was. He said, 'Call the boys, the company is marching at once'."

Ebenezer was instantly a man of action. Great walls of fire, he thought!

"Go get 'em, Ruth! You know where they are. They're picking up rocks on the new part of the lower field back of the house. They may be over the ridge near to the brook by now. I'll take a horse and get Jacob. He'll be up at his place." Over his shoulder as he raced for the barn he added, "Tell 'em to get out the other horse and get their muskets and powder."

Time seemed to stand still. Ben and Oliver came from the field on the run in answer to Ruthie's call and met her at the lower side of the mowing where the freshly worked land joined the field. Ruthie was breathless with sun hat in hand; her dress was spattered with mud, and she could only repeat what she had told Ebenezer.

When Ede joined up with her brothers, they questioned her as to the identity of the strange messenger. She had been struggling to keep up with her older sister, but her shorter legs had left her far behind. Equally frightened and nearly in tears, she only shook her head and muttered, "Oh, that poor horse!" Her concern for the rider's horse prompted Ben to ask if they had ever seen the horse before; both girls shook their heads.

Oliver, taking a cue from Ben, and hoping to identify either the horse or rider, asked what color the horse was.

Instantly, Ede replied, "White."

"Oh, no," contradicted Ruth, "It was brown."

"It was not," said Ede, "It was white with a few brown spots."

"Now I see what she means," Ruth interrupted. "Really it was a red or brown horse but white with sweat. He had been pushed really hard."

"Well, never mind about it any more. Hurry Ben, let's go. . . hurry!"

Followed by their younger sisters, the two brothers, half running with shirt tails flying raced up the field toward the house where Sarah and the younger children were waiting for them. Sarah, busy in the kitchen, felt the urgency of the moment. A chill ran down her spine, and for one brief moment she shivered despite the warmth of the day.

Excitement hung in the air like an ominous black cloud in the sky, heralding a torrential storm. Although Sarah had not seen the messenger, she had heard terror in the voices and had seen the girls run past the house and across the field. Both girls were crying now, and Sarah could not get satisfactory answers to her questions until they were safely in the house again. Little information came from Ede, who could only murmur above her muffled sobs, "Oh, that poor horse!"

Learning of the call to arms, Sarah with Ruthie's help went to work preparing food for each of the men to take along, bread, cheese and dried lamb. Oliver had gone at once to ready a horse. Ben assembled their muskets, horns and pouches.

Hoof beats outside, followed by a shout, brought Sarah to the door where Ebenezer sat astride one of his big horses with Jacob mounted behind him. Ebenezer's lusty shouts directed at no one in particular ordered someone, anyone, "Bring me my musket, hurry up!"

Ben rushed out the door carrying all three weapons. Everyone seemed to ignore Sarah's repeated pleas, "Ebenezer, you can't go. Ebenezer, someone has to stay here. You don't belong to the company. Lord, help us. What shall I do?"

After a brief but tearful farewell, two horses bearing four men, four muskets with the usual accouterments, passed from view over the knoll to what fate or glory no one knew.

News of the advance of the British troops reached the village of Groton early during the morning of April 19th when word was sent at once to all parts of the town calling on the Minutemen to rally on the Common. The alarm probably was a continuation of the one sent from Charlestown just before midnight and that reached Groton soon after sunrise. The speed with which the news traveled suggested that messengers stood ready to carry the word to the outlying farms.

As early as 1774 it had been voted that all able-bodied men purchase an iron field piece and ammunition. It was also in 1774 that a Convention of Blacksmiths for Worcester County was signed by forty three members resolving not to do any blacksmith work for the Tories or anyone in their employ. This moment had been anticipated and prepared for.

Sarah Patch sat in the kitchen chair nearest the door, her face buried in her trembling hands. About her stood all that was left of her family, four small children. Bewilderment, fear, shock, grief, each emotion showed on these little faces that but only a few minutes before were as carefree and as happy as is a child's right.

* * *

Jacob found that it was tricky business, keeping his seat behind Ebenezer on a horse that was being frantically urged to its fullest speed. That he also held two muskets, two powder horns and two bullet pouches compounded his frustration. Ben, seated behind Oliver, had an additional responsibility. As he left the kitchen, his mother had placed in his hands four substantial packages of meat and bread that he had silently vowed not to break open or to lose. He had thrust them inside his shirt before mounting the horse; and now with both hands needed to hold their firearms and pouches, he could not spare a hand to shift the packages to a safer, more comfortable position.

Bless her heart, he thought. When will we have time to eat on a day like this and under what conditions. We're going to have a lively time pushing those Redcoats, or lobsters as they were called by some, back to Boston and aboard their ships. It's got to be done though so we had best be at it. And aloud, "Oliver, can't you push him along any faster?"

In all New England towns, the church or meeting house was the people's only public building, and therefore the green in front of the church was today's meeting place. Sometimes called by the more general term, common, the green was also the place where the militia had trained on happier days when the recruits' families and neighbors turned out to watch the drill. Once rectangular in shape, it was now shaped more like a triangle as its corners had long ago been cut off by the wheels of turning ox carts.

On this solemn morning it was a place of frenzied turmoil. The officers of Groton's four military companies were frantically attempting to organize their commands. At the same time the town selectmen, standing on the steps in front of the church, were hastily doling out powder, bullets and flints. The town's stock was stored in the powder house, a twelve-foot square building located behind the meeting house. The responsibility fell to the selectmen on behalf of the town to provide and equip, from time to time, the town's quota of men and to furnish supplies of clothing and provisions as well as to provide for the support of the families of those who had gone to fight.

The men of the companies slowly wandered about chatting with friends and acquaintances, most dressed in the same manner with their long, brown deer skin leggings or homespun pants tucked in below the knee. Some wore low shoes with oversized buckles; others wore broad-brimmed felt hats, their powder horns slung over their shoulders. Some were without coats but wore sleeveless vests over handcrafted long-sleeved shirts.

Greeting each other, as friends, relatives and neighbors, they shook their powder horns to estimate contents, counting bullets and swapping stories about what each believed to be the true state of emergency. Some said that it was Edmund Bancroft who rode into town, bringing the word that the British were coming and that the towns folk nearer Boston were arming to meet them.

Through the preceding years, frequent Indian attacks had schooled Groton men in the arts of war. The trials of one horrifying campaign had prepared them for the duties of the next unfriendly encounter. Many of the men on the green about to serve their country had received their experience in warfare during the French and Indian War. All, like those generations of early Massachusetts settlers before them, had become familiar with the use of powder, ball and musket in their pursuit of game and other wild animals. Even young boys were skilled marksmen. Nearly 150 years earlier men were instructed to be ready at "halfe an howers warning."

Three citizens had been chosen to manage town affairs for the year: Doctor Oliver Prescott, Isaac Farnsworth and Amos Lawrence. Doctor Prescott was the younger brother of Colonel William Prescott and was the most noted as well as the most influential and celebrated man in Groton. A graduate of Harvard College in 1750, he was a member of various scientific societies, but most of all he was beloved by everyone in Groton for his gentle manner and kindly demeanor when caring for the sick.

Each man, who believed that he lacked sufficient ammunition for the mission, stood in line and received whatever was needed. Ebenezer and Benjamin, knowing their supplies were low, stepped into line, where Ebenezer was given a quarter pound of powder and twelve bullets, and Benjamin received one half pound of powder and twenty bullets. While Doctor Prescott was recording the transaction, Amos Lawrence approached Ebenezer, "Mr. Patch, I don't think we can allow you to go with the companies."

Ebenezer indignantly, "I am volunteering. I'm a Minuteman! I'm not militia." Ebenezer glanced at Doctor Prescott and Mr. Farnsworth. Each averted his gaze, both allowing themselves to be distracted by the tasks at hand. Ebenezer admonished, "I only want to defend our homes from the Redcoats, Amos."

It had been on October 26, 1774, that the First Provincial Congress of Massachusetts had resolved that the field officers of the various militia regiments enlist at least one-quarter of their respective commands and form into companies to be held in readiness to march at the shortest notice. Minutemen constituted that elite group of well-trained, well-organized individuals who could be called upon in that manner. The militia, also known as a body of training bands, was comprised of all other men folk, exclusive of old men and young boys, and was a less well organized group.

Everyone was in a hurry. The line behind Ebenezer was pushing and muttering. Mr. Lawrence with a conciliatory gesture offered, "Ebenezer, we are not as young as we once were. We can become part of the home guard."

Meanwhile Jacob and Oliver hurried a few rods past the church to the stone powder house standing on Benjamin Bancroft's land to stare at three brass cannon lying on the grass beside the magazine being guarded by two local men. These cannon, it was rumored, were brought to town the evening before by teams said to have come from Concord. No one could remember having seen them in town before.

The sight of these gigantic weapons resting at the ready in Groton had a sobering effect on those who viewed them. No one seemed to know for sure why they had been sent to town, and the mystery surrounding the whole affair and the rumors associated with their arrival were unpleasant omens none could deny. Their presence only served to enhance the sense of urgency and unrest among the crowd on the common.

One of the first reports the Patch men heard on reaching the common was that the recently appointed colonel of the Minutemen, William Prescott of Pepperell, had already passed through town on horseback after leaving orders for the Pepperell and Hollis men to meet him in Groton. Prescott was a commanding figure, unusually tall and exceeding well-proportioned, with sparkling deep blue eyes and a large head. He usually wore a skull cap but today had donned a tri-cornered hat. He always wore his thick hair parted in the middle, and he wore it long behind, braided loosely and tied with a thin, black ribbon. He was known by all to be extremely pleasant and polite, remarkably social and full of fun.

Now appear the Pepperell Minutemen marching rapidly at an extraordinarily fast pace set by James Lakin, the drummer, with John Nutting, Captain. Shouts of angst arose. This will never do. Pepperell ahead of Groton? Hurry! Come, let's go! This perceived humiliation brought order out of confusion. The company officers were nudging stragglers into line. Old men and boys ringed the common . In the background a few women and girls from nearby homes stood, many openly weeping. Words of advice, encouragement, cheer, endearment and courage hung in the anticipatory air, like pollen from the early spring flowers nearby.

The officers of Henry Farwell's company of Minutemen held a brief religious ceremony just before marching away. Prayers for safety and success for their cause were spoken in strong, clear voices.

Jacob took his place with Josiah Sartell's company, and Benjamin and Oliver fell in line in their company that was commanded by Captain Asa Lawrence. When all were ready, the Groton companies began to step out to confront the unseen enemy and undertake an unknowable adventure, the outcome of which no man could even guess. Henry Farwell's company led at a pace set by Joel Jenkins, company fifer.

Well, there they go, thought Ebenezer as he quickly strode across the common, or green as it was called, in front of the church to watch as the last of the Minutemen marched out of sight to the beat of drums. It was quiet now. The exodus was final and complete. The noise of youthful excitement had ceased, and the air became hollow and dull and empty. The uncomfortable parting of men had been abrupt and undemonstrative although the men lingered with their women until the last possible moment. All of a sudden Ebenezer felt lonely. It was not yet noon.

The only visible signs of recent turmoil were marks from the nervous tread of many anxious boots on the fresh new sprouts of pale yellow-green grass now turning to mud as the ground still held onto its moisture from winter's snow melt. Voices came from the church where selectmen were packing up what remained of the town's stock of powder and ball to be returned to the powder house. From Mr. Cutler's store next beyond the church came an uproarious mixture of voices, everyone trying to talk at once above all the rest, a real hullabaloo.

Renewed shouts coming closer caused Ebenezer to look back over his shoulder up the road toward the store at a running figure rapidly approaching. Above the cacophony of voices he was able to pick out the words "Abel Parker from Pepperell." A slightly winded man, musket in one hand and coat in the other, was abreast of the common now. The only sign of recognition was a fleeting smile on the face of the otherwise stern and serious Pepperell Minuteman. He pushed to increase his speed and was soon out of sight past the Prescott place. The congregation of voices stilled, and an eerie quiet settled once again over the village.

By the side of the now well-worn road at the foot of the green stood Ebenezer Patch, alone now, long musket in hand, standing straight and strong, feet braced in a defiant, determined manner, his knee-length gray coat hanging loosely around his shoulders. Too old, they had told him. Must stay home. Tried to make him think it would be an honor to be one of the "home guard." Home guard, indeed. Well perhaps his legs did tire before the end of the day, but believe you me, he would never admit it. May a maple log roll over me! His hand was steady, and his eye, keen.

Later on, the town would prepare an alarm list, a list of those persons too young (under eighteen) or too old (over fifty) to endure the hardships of war. These individuals, it was believed, in an emergency or as a home guard, could provide efficient service. In fact it was on the 24th of April 1775 that Groton's Doctor Oliver Prescott sent the following to the Committee of Safety: "Gentlemen. I think if an order should pass for the establishment of a Town Guard, to be kept in a prudent manner, in every town in the Province, it would have a great tendency to deter and detract villains and their accomplices. The passes that people bring this way are generally without dates, or assignment to any person or place, so that a man may pass to—with the same order. Pardon my freedom and allow me to subscribe, gentlemen, your most obedient, very humble servant." (Signed) Oliver Prescott.

The weight of the ammunition pouch hung heavy now with the addition of twelve more newly issued bullets. Ebenezer's hand dropped, and, without thinking, he made the familiar gesture of all men who have ever carried a powder horn, feeling to see that the stopper was secure. Must have had quite a bit, he thought, as it took only a quarter pound to fill it.

Anger stirred in him again. Too old? In a pig's eye! It was not just what Amos Lawrence said, but it was what he meant. No doubt about it. All this war business had turned Amos's head. Why Amos was even older than me, by let's see, four or five years at least. Amos used to be a pretty sensible man, but something was wrong with him today for sure. Old, hey? Ask the boys who put the ridge boards on the roof of the new house. And in spite of all the argument, they would not let him go. Brother Isaac had his chance in the French war and was clear up to Crown Point. This was my last chance to go with my three boys!

Relaxing a bit, he stood by the roadside, desolate and alone. He repositioned his felt hat, brushing a few strands of gray blond hair back over his ears toward the nape of his neck where it was tied. How long had he been standing so, this lone figure in the tepid, yellow sunlight. Ebenezer heard the last faint, shrill martial notes of the eerie fife as it rounded the last curve behind Indian Hill on the road to the Bay. He was tired, and a weariness descended upon him. The pressure in his chest that had been nagging him cut his breath. The musket in his gray-coated arms felt heavy, and his arms drooped dispassionately to his sides.

Just you wait, they will need me before this is over. This is just the beginning. He could feel it. He would go home and get things in shape so that Sarah and Mary, yes, and Ruthie too, could care for the stock for a bit when he was called next to go with his boys. Start right now. Where are the horses?

Ebenezer, visibly crestfallen, worried as never before and stunned by the sudden although not entirely unexpected events, walked slowly up the gently sloping common to the church. A number of unattended horses slowly roamed about, looking for any sustenance in the uninviting ground. The throng about the store had dispersed. Being in no mood to seek company and thinking only of getting home as soon as possible, Ebenezer took a last look at the scene of recent ferment and walked on past the church. Half way down the hill and also headed home, Ebenezer's horses grazed tentatively on last year's dead grass. Responsibility for his animals eased the tension of the moment.

A short while later Ebenezer slowly rode into his yard leading the second horse. Flinging himself to the ground, he burst into the kitchen, "Sarah, they have gone! Three of our boys have gone."

Chapter VI

ASHBY

April 19th promised to be another splendid spring day, warm and bright, with a cerulean sky free of even a whisper of cloud. Now new green growth was beginning to appear everywhere. Simon wondered, somewhat fancifully, if one by careful observation might actually be able to see the new grass increase in length as it stretched up to the warming sun. How could there be trouble anywhere when the sky was so blue and the air so balmy? It seemed hard to believe, but there was trouble, make no mistake. Constantly hovering in the background was that uneasy, restless something. It had been so for some time now.

Simon was fully aware of the alarming condition of the affairs of the colony. He had been as busy as a cub bear with a hornet's nest and way too busy to leave home for any stretch of time except on very pressing matters. News was several days old when he heard it from his cousin, Stephen, who was a member of Captain Samuel Stone's Minuteman Company and regularly attended drill sessions in Ashby.

Simon had cleared nearly all of the stumps and mid-sized stones from the new field where he hoped to plant soon. Remaining were only a few big boulders. To remove them was a challenge requiring that he and Stephen "double up." Any rock that resisted the animal power of both teams working simultaneously would be left for another time. Then the immovable boulder would either be buried in a deep pit or split with wedges into foundation stones for later building. Today Stephen would be helping him.

Another pesky crow gone, thought Simon, hearing far in the distance a musket shot. Sounds as far away as Pepperell. Thinking of crows led his mind to corn for which they have a great fondness. This in turn brought up the dilemma of how much of his land he would allot to corn and how much to rye and wheat.

The still air brought the sound of another shot. Good, another one gone. Why don't we declare a crow day when everyone could spend a whole day ridding the town of crows. In the spring of 1645 the General Court had ordered that all youths ages ten to sixteen would be instructed by competent soldiers in the exercise of firearms—small guns, half pikes and bows and arrows, providing their parents were willing. Perhaps boys were practicing this morning on the crows, he thought.

Time slips by quickly when one's mind is pleasantly occupied, and the increasing warmth of the ascending sun brought Simon from his reverie. Why, the sun is getting high, almost noon, where is Stephen? We have quite a job ahead of us today. I had best go and see what is keeping him; perhaps he had trouble of some kind. Great Caesar's suspenders! Another shot and nearer too. While cutting across the field to the path that led to his cousin's house, he heard yet another shot echoing up the hill from Townsend way. Passing through the woods and nearing Stephen's field came a shot from the Trap Falls section just to the north. Now it was plain to see that the shots had been spaced into time intervals and that the firing had progressed from east to west.

Bursting out of the woods and onto the field in front of Stephen's house, the first oddity catching Simon's eye was that both of the oxen were placidly nibbling tender new grass. Their yoke lay beside the path, the bows scattered. Muttering to himself as he stepped over one of the bows, Simon saw that one of Stephen's highly prized bow-pins had been embedded in the soft earth by the heel of a hurrying boot, the footprint still visible in the soft soil. He stooped to retrieve the bow-pin, opining that Stephen must have been in a real sweat to have dropped the pins in the mud as he did. He always said they were the finest pins he ever had.

Rushing up to the house where the door stood ajar, Simon stepped inside, and a hasty glance told him that the silent house was empty. Turning he looked behind the kitchen door where a musket always stood in the corner. It was gone.

"Well, may I be chased by tom cats," he exclaimed out loud. One leap and he was out of the door running down the well-trodden path toward home. The startled oxen gazed in surprise for a moment and then returned to grazing.

Elizabeth had gone outdoors in time to hear the nearby shots. Her usual placid, unruffled appearance belied a high-strung and worrisome nature. Anxiety had mounted these last few weeks. She felt concern over Simon's ambitious plans for the future. Stephen's detailed reports about prevailing political unrest added tremendously to her uneasiness. There was truly something frightening about these shots spaced so evenly in time and apparent location. Hands clasped together, Elizabeth paced back and forth on the hard-packed earth close by the house, awaiting some indication from Simon. Plainly something was terribly amiss. Whatever it was what could she do about it? She felt helpless.

Minutes dragged, but at last she saw him trotting toward her. She ran to meet him, crying out as she ran, "Simon! What's wrong? What's happened? Simon!"

Standing in the middle of the field, he told her about hearing the shots that sent him speeding to Stephen's house. Breathlessly he told her of the grazing oxen, the scattered bow and pins and of the deserted house and missing musket. Quickly he told her what it all probably meant.

They stood, hands clasped, not speaking, looking at the ground, wrapped in the thought of the enormity of what was likely happening. Slowly they started to walk back toward the house. Repeatedly they told each other what they had seen and heard. Separately they set forth their ideas as to its significance.

Jointly they expressed their hopes, and together they affirmed their cautious belief in their own now tentative future. Quietly now, they stood on the area of dry earth before their door. Simon looking off to the southeast, imagined that he could hear the squeal of frantic fifes and the tedium rattle of drums resounding above the boom of muskets. In his mind's eye he could see his friends and brothers marching, marching, marching into what he could not see, a vague endless tunnel of emptiness.

Elizabeth stood beside him, looking toward a fancied location which might be Boston although she had never been further from her childhood home than where she was at that very moment. She could in her imagination hear the thump and then the tearing sound as a musket ball smashed through an already tattered coat into soft young flesh beneath. In her imagery she saw screaming young men, her brothers, perhaps, throw up their grasping arms and fall, sprawling haphazardly and silent to the ground.

Standing thus, Simon and Elizabeth, transfixed by the horror of their individual thoughts, were brought back into the reality of the moment by little Rebecca, whose footsteps followed the bang of the cottage door and her childish voice piping, "Mama, Nathan is on the table playing with your best plates. Mama, what are you looking at? Mama, can't you hear him banging your best plates together?"

"My foot! You go and make him get down! Go this instant. I will be there in a couple of minutes. Go now!" Elizabeth, turning to face her husband, "Simon, just think what this means. You may have to go. Probably you will. Whatever will I do? I could go home. Probably my brothers will all go too. And father dead but four months. No! I want to stay here. Someone must stay here anyway. I know! Maybe I can get great Aunt Elizabeth Lakin to come and stay with me. There are ever so many Lakins living close by each other there on the Throne. They can get along without an old woman like Aunt Elizabeth for a while. She could tend to the children while I do your work. Simon, I'm frightened! Say something quickly before I scream!"

"Indeed I will," he said as he leaned over and kissed his beautiful Elizabeth. "Now I must go and and look after Stephen's cattle."

History would record that the alarm that aroused the Ashby Minutemen was fired about nine o'clock in the morning. It likely was fired in front of the house of Lt. Jonas Barrett who was an inn holder and second in command of the Minute Men. Within a short time this company of forty six men under the command of Captain Samuel Stone shouldered their muskets and hurried toward the scene of action becoming part of Colonel William Prescott's Regiment. Samuel Stone Jr. was the fifer, and Timothy Stone, the drummer. Stephen Patch was a member of that company.

Chapter VII

PRUDENCE WRIGHT

The days following the departure for Concord of the four Groton military companies were hectic and trying ones for Ebenezer; the strains and excitement of that day were but the beginning. He knew little or nothing of the news of the day beyond hearing that the Groton companies had not arrived in time to take part in the battle but were perhaps involved in later skirmishes. The latest he had heard was that the Congress had voted to increase the Bay Colony's military force to 13,000 men, a tremendous number and cause for an endless flock of new worries. First, his boys would not be back for a very long time. How would work at home progress without them. To compound his growing dismay, the needed man power might be found without a call for him to enlist; and, therefore, the chance to serve his country would be lost forever.

He had been on the run from day break until nightfall. All chores on this farm were now his responsibility alone. Daily he climbed the hill to Jacob's house to do whatever must be done there to help Mary. Several times in his loneliness and frustration he had gone over to the Hazens. He had made several feeble attempts to begin work on an ambitious plan for creating an enlarged vegetable garden, but after an hour or so he had suspended work, promising himself an earlier start the next day. Sometimes he would go to town hoping to somehow hear something of the boys.

Today on his return to the house, his first glimpse of the yard revealed a strange horse tied to the post near his back door.

"Who in Tophet may that be?" he thought aloud, anxiously urging his horse along. Upon entering his kitchen he found the surprise visitor to be David Wright of Pepperell, a second cousin of his wife, Sarah.

"Glad to see you, David. Nothing wrong with your people? No bad news, I hope. How did you get to be here?"

"Well, Ebenezer, it's like this. I have been wantin' to get over to Westford to see the folks ever since the snow went out. You well know how things have been. So today I just started out. I came over the bridge above Blood's ford way and followed that road down through Unquity and up over Horse Hill, stopped and spoke with Jacob's wife. When I leave here I'll go back towards Dunstable and take that old road to the mill site on the brook down at your lower boundary, then across the brook and on into Westford that way. I shan't go up over Chestnut Hill, I'll keep to the right and go past Long Sought For Pond. It's about as near as the main road, and I wanted to see Sarah and tell you folks about the doin's in Pepperell."

"I see," remarked Ebenezer, not particularly interested in David's itinerary for the day.

"Well, land sakes, David, you had gotten through with all that before Ebenezer came in. Hurry up and tell us of these doings," said Sarah.

"All right, I'll tell it as fast as I can," David replied, taking a deep breath and making a new start.

"You both know how Prudence is, full of fire and energy. You know about those snapping black eyes of hers! Well, since the trouble started, she has gotten together a lot of women who say that they are going to protect the town from the regulars after all the men folks of Pepperell have gone into this new army that's gettin' up. Prudence thinks there should be a town guard for women like the men have. She has got the women folk all stirred up. There's thirty or forty of them! They know that the men folks helped chase the British and are now with the other Minute Men near Boston. They heard that spies have been passin' between the British in Canada and them ones in Boston. One direct road runs right through Pepperell!"

David paused to catch his breath, "There are even some Groton women joined up with her too. I know at least two from Groton. Job Shattuck's wife, she was a Hartwell, I think. They live just across the river from Pepperell anyway and Quarles, Susannah it is—she's the wife of the baker, I hear. I guess Pepperell got the jump on Groton this time all right."

"May I be chased by the tomcats! Women!" said Ebenezer weakly.

"Well," continued David, "It seems—say did you ever hear of a man in Hollis named Leonard Whiting? Well, you know Prudence's brothers, Sam and Thomas. It seems that they are not with us. That is, they go along with the Tory crowd. I am ashamed to say it, but they do sure enough, but her youngest brother, Ben, is with us all right. He belongs to Captain Ruben Dow's Minutemen of Hollis. That's part of Colonel William Prescott's Regiment, ya know."

"Well, for conscience sake, what happened?" snapped Ebenezer. "Don't beat around any longer."

"Sure, sure, where did I leave off. You know, they, these women folk I mean, call Prudence their commander," David chuckled. "Oh, yes, about Leonard Whiting. You know he has for some time been an officer in the King's army. He is the one that got Sam and Tom into this by taking them to meetings over at what they call Tory Tavern. It's over in Townsend. Then there's a lawyer up in Hollis named Samuel Cutts Shannon who is in on it too. I blame him most of all. He moved down here from Portsmouth not very long ago. I'll bet they drove him out of Portsmouth."

Sarah was not a talkative woman, but at last she impatiently broke in, "David, did anything really happen in Pepperell, or didn't it? Tell us!"

"Oh, yes! Sure, sure did. Well, as I was saying, "I don't believe there is anyone anywhere who believes in our cause more'n Prudence does. She was one of the very first to throw our tea onto the fire the night they had the bonfire in front of the church and burned up all the tea in town. Pepperell was the first to do it. First to put up a liberty pole, too. Got ahead of you folks that time too. Why, I really think she would have gone to Concord with Captain Nuttings Minute Company if he'd have let her."

"Thunder, " snorted Ebenezer.

"David!" said Sarah.

"Well, to go on," resumed David, "You know when Edmund Bancroft came ridin' into town that morning, shoutin' just as loud as he could that fightin' had broke out, and some of our men had been killed in Concord. . . Well, that set Prudence off. She has spent most all of her time since then molding bullets and the like and workin' with her home guard."

"Home guard," shouted Ebenezer and then muttered to himself. Home guard. There it goes again. Me and the women. Home guard. Well upon my soul!

"What'd you say?" inquired David mildly. "Oh, well, never mind. It seems that she heard that Whiting was to bring some kind of a message from some of the King's men in Canada to some general or other in Boston. Well, sir, Prudence got her women together and that took some ridin' around, I'll tell you. She was even wearin' my clothes! Ebenezer, you know there at the bridge, the one I just come over, Jewett's over the Nashua River, how that ledge on the north side sticks out into the road sort of? Kind of hides the bridge so that you come onto it sort of quick like. And you remember that on the south side there are those big old pine trees? Well, them women had muskets and clubs and spears and I don't know what all else, pitch forks even, and went and hid in those big pines, and about dark they hears two horses coming. Yes sir, sure did. There's no houses around there, you know."

"Oh, my soul and body!" exclaimed Sarah.

"Well, just as them horses was about to step off the bridge from the north, the women rose up and jumped out and stopped them. Yes, sir, they sure did. One of the pair of rascals turned back and got away. They caught the other one, and sure enough it was Whiting all right. Prudence told him to get down off that horse so he could be searched, and I guess he did what he was told 'cause they found the papers in his boot, they did. They took Whiting, a-whining and a-fussing like all get-out right up Main Street to Solomon Rogers's Tavern and guarded him there all night. In the morning they took him to Groton and delivered him and the papers to Oliver Prescott. Mr. Prescott sent the papers to the Committee of Safety in Charlestown."

"Well I snum," said Ebenezer. "I did hear that Mr. Prescott had a prisoner penned up somewhere, but no one was sure who it was."

"You were right, David. Things have been happening in Pepperell," demurred Sarah, "And I hope you realize what a wonderful wife you have."

David continued, "Did you know that Prudence's brother, Tom, hasn't been seen or heard of since that day. I'm bettin' that he was the one that got away. He and Whiting were great cronies, you know. I don't know whatever happened to Whiting, but I wager he won't come around these parts no more. Say, I've worked on Prudence every minute that she is at home, tryin' to get her to tell me how she found out about Whiting coming through town with those papers. All she will say is 'I have spies all 'round.' I think she may have overhead somethin' somewhere. They say the Loyalists meet in Tory Tavern in Townsend Harbor. It's not unthinkable that she may have heard somethin' her brothers may have said. Makes a man kind of jumpy. She won't tell me anything. I don't dare say much or ask any more questions. If I did, she would pick me all apart to find out more. I hear that Doctor Prescott is working on some kind of an order that will make everyone travelin' the roads have a pass, and they will have to show it to some of the town guard in every town.

"Ebenezer, what ails you. What makes you wince like that?" David continued with a laugh, "I suppose I could get one, and I would have to show it to Prudence every time I went anywhere! What will we have next? If I travel such roads as the one I am travelin' today, I guess no one will stop me. All I've seen so far is one of them Blood boys up by Unquity and Jacob's wife. She said all your boys went to Concord except Simon. Living way up there, he didn't know, like as not. Probably we'll all go before it is over. Well, I have got to get moving. Must hurry home by way of Westford and see what new thing Prudence is up to. I guess we won't have much chance to visit around much for quite a spell, the way things look."

As David stood up and moved toward the door, Sarah gave him messages for various Wrights in Westford and a special message for Prudence also. Sarah was very fond of Prudence and had great admiration for her. She knew that when Prudence was eighteen years old she could spin, weave and dye linen and woolen cloths. Prudence knew the process by which flax and fleece became completed garments. She could knit. She could dip and mold candles, mold bullets and buck shot and make pewter spoons. She could handle a flintlock. She could walk in snow shoes and ride a horse. She knew the process for preserving meats. She could make soap, braid mats and make hats. She was also an accomplished cook and could boil cider, make apple jack and boil sap into syrup and sugar. There was not much she could not do.

Ebenezer murmured words of praise and encouragement for Prudence and her spies.

As David rode out of the yard, Ebenezer closed the door and said, "For conscience sake, what do you think of all that?"

Sarah said, "I guess Prudence runs the Wright household for sure."

Ruthie's first and only comment was, "I think Prudence is wonderful."

Chapter VIII

THE AFTERMATH

Ever since early childhood Benjamin had been very fond of all animals, but more especially of dogs. For many years he had been privileged to have the companionship of one favorite in particular. A couple of years before this story begins, old age claimed the life of his friend. Benjamin was heart broken by this loss, and not a day passed when he didn't think about this lost creature.

On an unbelievably cold and windy winter night the following year after finishing the evening chores, Benjamin pushed open the barn door against the wind and prepared to make a dash across the bridle path to the house. He found the roadway barred by a young, scrawny, short-haired brown dog who arose wagging his tail expectantly. Startled, but not immediately interested, Benjamin stepped aside and holding the door open, said, "Why, hello, come right in," and added as an after thought the first name that came to mind, "George."

The furry visitor immediately accepted the kindly invitation and the next morning showed no inclination to be on his way. No one in the neighborhood knew of any lost dogs, so George stayed on. Some of Benjamin's friends, most of whom were Minutemen, jokingly accused him of naming his new friend in honor of the monarch, George III. Others said it was done in derision, lowering his Majesty to the equal rank of a canine. Many who were dog lovers said it was too fine an animal to be given such an opprobrious name. However, Ben continued to insist that it was the first name to enter his mind at the moment of their first meeting.

A close and satisfying man-dog relationship grew between them, and none of the family suffered greater anguish in the days since the boys went away than did George. He had been Benjamin's constant companion now for more than a year, and his master's inexplicable absence seemed like abject desertion. Most of each day and into the evening George spent lying close to the young ash tree in front of the house. This was a vantage point giving the best view of the road over which Benjamin had ridden away.

April dragged along. People in the Bay Colony lived in a constant state of expectancy and fear. Rumors of every kind flooded the area. Stories brought to town by those who, for one reason or another, came from the vicinity of Boston were tales of confusion and disarray. Most customary travel between towns had ceased, but a number of people had journeyed to Cambridge, carrying food, clothing and arms to some beloved son or father; and almost always they were loaded down with similar articles from neighbors. In addition, increasing demands were made upon each town to supply food and clothing for the growing army.

April finally gave way to May, and the fourth day of the new month was drawing to a close when the early evening quiet of the Patch homestead was shattered by an uproar in front of the house, not a bark and not a howl but a low-pitched bellow from deep within George's throat.

"Land sakes, Ede," said Sarah who was in the midst of preparing supper, "Run and see what has got into that dog! I never heard such a noise!"

Ede ran to the front of the house and looking westerly into the brilliant sunset to the stony rise over which the road passed, saw outlined in gold against a flaming sky, the silhouette of a man, a musket and a dog, man and dog engrossed in joyful reunion. Ede's young voice, aquiver with excitement, exuberantly proclaimed to the world the news, "It's Ben! Ben's coming home!"

After Benjamin had greeted each member of the family, and they in turn exclaimed their profound gratitude for his safe return, thanks to the Almighty, he explained that none of the boys in the family or in the neighborhood had been injured so far as he knew. He began his story. He along with Jacob, Benjamin Hazen and Daniel Williams, Elizabeth's brother, marched from Cambridge in a group as far as "The Ridges." There Daniel joined with another group that had come up to them and continued on into town. On the march home and before Benjamin and Daniel parted ways, Daniel agreed to go tomorrow to visit Simon, carrying the news and giving his sister, Elizabeth, assurance that all was well.

Benjamin related that he, along with Jacob and Ben Hazen, had turned east just above "The Ridges" and followed the woods path around Cow Pond across the Westford road and on to the Hazen home near the brook. Jacob had stopped to bring along some things that Mrs. Hazen wanted to send to Mary, and he would join them shortly.

Everyone had a question. Ebenezer wanted to know what action they had been in. Sarah worried until he told her that he had not been hurt in any way and had had enough to eat. Ruth wondered, ". . .what those awful Britishers looked like."

Ede whispered, "Did you see that poor white horse anywhere?"

Sammy kept shouting, "Did you kill any Redcoats?"

Benjamin related that the Groton companies had seen no action. The battle had rolled on toward Charlestown about as fast as they themselves had progressed. He said that the Groton companies had spent the night in a field somewhere near the Lexington-Menotomy (Arlington) line and that early the next morning had moved along quickly, following the chaos and destruction of battle almost to Charlestown where they were turned back and directed to Cambridge where the American army would become headquartered.

Many men believed that General Thomas Gage would march out from Boston the very next day with a superior force, and then a real battle would take place. General Gage, Governor of Massachusetts and British Military Governor, several months earlier had undertaken a mission to destroy the military arms stored in Salem but subsequently retreated, not succeeding in his attempt. Later he was charged with destroying the store of military armaments in Concord, and it was he who had occupied Boston with British troops. His attempt to enforce the Intolerable Acts in response to the Boston Tea Party inflamed the colonists, and they were understandably extremely wary of him.

For this reason a large number of American militia and Minutemen were posted on guard duty. The area near and about Harvard College was a seething mass of volunteer troops with more arriving all through the day and into the night, converging there from every outlying region. When Benjamin had left the day before, there were men from Rhode Island, Connecticut, New Hampshire, New York and even New Jersey, and more were still coming. Some were well ordered and equipped; many others were only groups of eager young men without adequate clothing, without officers in authority and many, armed only with anything that came to hand. Many men's trades could be learned by the weapons they carried; in some cases the only weapon was a knife, a hammer or perhaps an ax. Warfare was not their occupation.

The Groton boys had been assigned to guard duty and to directing incoming groups. Benjamin related that Oliver had enlisted for ninety eight days on April 25th when the Groton companies merged. He hoped that it met with Ebenezer's approval. He and Jacob had thought it best to come home for a family conference before signing up, but both felt that they had a duty to perform and that a decision of what would be best would have to be made. He had seen Stephen only once and then for only the briefest of greetings.

In reply to Ebenezer's question about the seriousness of the battle and the dead and wounded, he responded, "Father, it was horrible. We saw little in Groton, but as we traveled on, evidence of death and destruction increased with every mile. The dead were lying by the roadside, and weeping families were searching in the adjacent fields and woods for the dead and injured. Houses and barns were in flame. The road was littered with discarded muskets, Redcoat uniforms and abandoned plunder that had been stolen from the houses the Redcoats had ransacked. We were under orders to make no stops. It was a forced march all the way.

"After Jacob and I agreed that we had best come home for a while, I planned that on the way home I would make a mental list of the things I had seen so that you would know what it was like. Knowing that you were born in Concord, I figured you would remember many of the people in those towns."

"I was a small boy when we left Concord," recalled Ebenezer quietly, "but I used to visit there with Father and through him knew many of the families. Tell me, Ben, just what did you see?"

All the while that Ben had been talking, he stroked the top of George's head. George sat beside his chair and still gave an occasional whimper as though asking for a greater share of his master's attention. Without looking up in response to Ebenezer's question, Ben stated emphatically, "I'll tell you there is just one dog in a lifetime, and this is the one for me." George looked up at Benjamin appreciatively.

"We met up with the other troops on the common in Cambridge, and the president of Harvard College offered a prayer. Of course there was no fighting in Cambridge where they were stationed, but in the northern part from where the Somerville road turns off until we reached the Menotomy (Arlington) line four Americans were killed and one Britisher. This is perhaps a distance of a mile and a half or two miles. One was Major Isaac Gardner of Brookline and another was a lad who was sitting on a fence watching and probably had no idea what it was all about.

"The town line is about where the road crosses Menotomy River. From that bridge until we reached Lexington was the worst. We stopped on the way home to talk with people whenever we could, and I managed to get some paper and a bit of graphite so I could write down some figures. There were more than forty Redcoats killed in Menotomy, and we lost twenty five there. A British wagon train loaded with food and supplies, heading for Concord, was way laid by a few of our old men who were helped by an Indian. They seized the horses and wagons and killed a number of the drivers and guards. Six of the guards escaped but later surrendered to our brave old women. Many of our people who were killed were old or lame and simply just going about their business. They were innocent victims.

"All through Menotomy there were burned and abandoned houses, many with doors and windows smashed, fences down, just plain destruction. Of course, it's now a little more than two weeks since the battle. This is May 4th, I think. I wanted to ask questions of some of the people we saw, but I didn't have the heart to bother them. There were no young men anywhere, only boys, feeble old men and a few women. They all looked so sad and were working so hard trying to patch up the houses that were worth fixing."

Ebenezer arose to restore the fire, his tired face strained by unspoken grief.

"Do you remember the Cooper Tavern?" Benjamin continued rhetorically, "A woman standing in the door yard told me she had counted 100 bullet holes in the walls. The fighting was very bad. Nearly twenty of our men and even more of the regulars fell there as well as several at the Tavern itself."

"Great balls of fire! Benjamin Cooper. I knew him. I've stopped there. His wife was Rachel," said Ebenezer in a low voice barely above a whisper.

"The troops that came along later in the day to reinforce the regulars brought a couple of cannon with them. Near the foot of Pierce's Hill by the big rocks they stopped and fired the cannon at many of the houses. No one could ever count the damage to the houses and furniture long about there, and I can't exactly describe it either," said Ben sadly.

Ebenezer arose from his chair, "If I had not been a copper-bottomed idiot, I would have gone along anyway in spite of what Amos Lawrence said. Go on, Benjamin, I want to hear the rest of it. None of us slept a wink that night after you boys left, and I am sure I won't sleep tonight." As if to reinforce this thought, Ebenezer began to pace the kitchen floor.

"Speaking of sleep, we didn't sleep that night either," continued Ben. "We stayed in a field at about the Menotomy and Lexington town line. If you remember, the moon had been nearly full for a few nights, and that night it was very bright, near as light as day."

"It rose at a quarter to ten that night," said Sarah. "I know because we were up and about all night. Your father took on something awful, Ben, and probably I was just as bad."

"Coming home, we didn't leave Cambridge very early. We decided to spend the night in the same field where we had stayed before. It's on the east side of the road just as you come to the Lexington town line," continued Ben, "It was quiet there; and as I lay in the grass in the darkness, I thought about the other night I had spent there just a couple of weeks before.

"The night after the battle we slept hardly at all. People were wandering through the fields hunting in the grass and in the brush along the walls for those thought to be missing. They were calling out various names, searching, I suppose, for someone who was missing or that in fright had run from home. Some were probably looking for the body of some Minuteman. Others had heard vague rumors that their loved one had been seen to fall during battle and had not been known to rise. In the stillness of a perfect night we could hear much of the talk of the searchers and of those passing on the road.

"All night the road was crowded with people leaving Cambridge and Menotomy. Many expected the whole British army would come out from Boston the next day and kill everyone they could find. Some were families whose homes had been burned or so badly violated as to be worthless. Very few had carts of any kind. They all carried as many of their possessions as possible. Some with heavy packs on their backs. Some carrying a choice piece of furniture. A few I thought had completely lost their minds. A few of the carts passed silently without a word spoken, and we knew that they would be carrying the body of some friend or relative who was to be buried in some safe, quiet spot away from the sound of cannon or marching regulars.

"These people all had one thing in common. They were trying to reach some safe place, perhaps deep in the woods somewhere or maybe the home of some friend or relative, perhaps up this way or maybe even in New Hampshire. Probably they had nothing to keep them from moving on as so many homes were practically destroyed. As we rested there yesterday, it almost seemed that I could hear those voices again, some sobbing, some cursing, some praying. . ."

Benjamin paused, perhaps to relive some scene, and the room was silent except for Sarah's muffled sobs, "Heavens to betsy, is there more? I cannot bear to hear of such things happening to our people just a few miles away. What if all this had happened in Groton?"

George stirred and moaned. Ebenezer stopped pacing the floor long enough to proclaim, "But for those brave men it would have! The Britishers would have come after those cannon we saw laying outside of our powder house. We are in it now, win or lose."

Ben was on his feet now too, and thinking out loud, continued, "Father is right, Mother. In Lexington the British seized the Munroe Tavern, shooting the barkeep in the back as he tried to move toward a safe place. It was bad between Munroe's and the green in Lexington. The British reinforcement company set up their cannon again in the field across from the widow Lydia Mulliken's and fired at the church on the green. One ball went right through, yes, sir, in the south wall and out the north wall. Pretty much wrecked it. The Mulliken house and blacksmith shop and another building where they made clock parts were all burned. Also Joseph Loring's buildings, as well as Joshua Bond's house.

"The first of our men killed was there on the green at daylight on the 19th as the regulars were marching toward Concord. Eight of Captain Parker's men were killed on the green in front of Buckman's Tavern, and ten were wounded. William Tidd was almost killed by a mounted officer. He saved his life by quickly stepping to one side and firing at close range. His brother, John, was one of the last to leave. He was struck on the head by the sword of another mounted officer which almost scalped him. He was left for dead and later robbed by one of the Redcoats, but they say John will be all right in time.

"From Lexington to Concord there was not so much damage, but many were killed, some near a big ledge at a curve in the road just before you enter the town of Concord. Another place where quite a number on both sides were killed and many were wounded was a stretch of woods between the Hartwell farms and the two brooks near what they call Brooks Hill."

"Yes, yes, I know the place," murmured Ebenezer.

"Near where the road turns off to Bedford at Mill Brook Bridge there was a lot of fighting. Probably you've heard that all the trouble in Concord began at the North Bridge over the river. Of course, we did not come that way so didn't see anything there.

"One thing I did learn that pleased me was what Doctor Samuel Prescott did. The night before the battle, the Committee of Safety in Boston send a warning message to Mr. Hancock and to Mr. Adams; they were staying in Lexington. The messengers, a Mr. Revere and Mr. Dawes brought notice of a possible invasion of Concord. By chance they met Doctor Prescott in Lexington who rode toward Concord with them. All three were captured by British officers on patrol. However, Doctor Prescott escaped by some miracle and notified Mr. Melvin, the town watchman in Concord of what was going on. This gave the Concord company time to get ready. By the way, Doctor Prescott had spent the evening visiting Lydia Mulliken who was the daughter of the family I just told you about whose house was burned.

"Oh, yes, do you know who brought us the alarm the morning that we marched? Well, it was Sam Lawrence or the man who works for his father, you know, Oliver Wentworth. I didn't see Sam to talk with so I don't know which one came down here."

Night fall had arrived by the time Benjamin's story was told, bringing shadows into the room shared at that moment by Ebenezer's family. George was lying in front of the fire with his head on Benjamin's foot, positioning himself to be alert to any movement in his master's body. Ruthie was leaning against the wall with her head dropped to her chest having fallen asleep to the drone of Benjamin's voice. Both Ede and Samuel were also asleep with their heads in Ruthie's lap. Sarah, Ebenezer and Benjamin sat silently deep in thought and drained from the emotions of the moment. It was time for bed. Tomorrow would be another day.

The citizens of Groton were often interrelated, and many had relatives in nearby towns. In fact, several of the town's early settlers were from Concord. Numerous families were related to those who were killed or injured on Concord's green. Even people 200 years later and several generations removed have not forgotten what happened there to distant cousins such as the Tidd brothers and Abel Prescott.

Although no resident of the town was injured, all felt themselves a part of this episode in history as they had been entrusted with the cannon and barrels of precious powder that had been removed from Concord. It was not known until much later that in addition to the cannon, Concord also had planned to send six medical chests, several yards of Russian linen and 157 tents for safekeeping, but as it turned out they were never actually sent.

It also later became known that a message was sent by Paul Revere on Sunday April 16, 1775, to the effect that the British were preparing for an incursion into the country, and it was at once understood that the stores and ammunition housed at Concord would be vulnerable to attack. Revere delivered his message promptly to Lexington and returned in the afternoon when he made arrangements with Colonel Conant about the signal lanterns in the church. Then he crossed the river from Charleston.

On the next day the Provincial Congress in Concord voted that the four six pounders be transported to Groton and placed under the care of Colonel Prescott. In accordance with the final votes of the Committee the next morning, the 18th, the cannon were promptly on their way to Groton and arrived there late in the afternoon.

In the days that followed, the Committee on Safety and the Provincial Congress continued their efforts to create structure and organization for the army using their collective experience in past conflicts and the European model as guides. They determined the size of regiments and companies and the numbers and types of leaders required. What they did not successfully resolve was the shortage of ammunition and the issue regarding coordination of leadership.

Chapter IX

LATE SPRING

More than twenty years had passed since Benjamin Franklin was appointed Postmaster General, yet by the time of the Revolution there were only a few post offices in the Province. Previously Franklin had personally laid out milestones on the post road between Philadelphia and Boston; and, it has been said, he drove over roads that were to be marked seated in a comfortable chaise. He was followed by a gang of men in carts loaded with milestones. Franklin marked off the miles using a piece of equipment or stick attached to the wheel of his chaise. After passing each mile, he halted, and a stone was dropped that was later set into the ground.

However, individuals in distant parts of the Bay Colony still received their correspondence in Boston, and no record has been found of any post rider passing through Groton during this period. The flow of information occurred slowly as the result of word of mouth, mostly from those individuals traveling between Boston and Groton, and news of more bloodshed continued to trickle in. British troops had settled into Boston, creating much anxiety among the local men. In addition there was the issue of what to do about Reverend Dana.

Reverend Dana's problems had begun in March when he preached a sermon supporting the British. The town folks were outraged. Just about everyone favored resistance to British tyranny under which they had been living now for many years.

We should have known about Dana, mused Ebenezer to himself. In March some of the towns people refused to sign the covenant agreed upon by the town and based upon the recommendation from Congress. At the March meeting of the "freeholders" in Groton it was voted that the names of those who refused to sign the Association paper be posted in the public houses and their names entered in the town book by the town clerk. Four individuals refused to sign the document including Reverend Samuel Dana.

* * *

At four o'clock in the afternoon Ebenezer was sitting at the sunlight kitchen table sipping a cup of bayberry tea, a custom he had developed when English tea no longer became available due to import restrictions. He was slowly becoming accustomed to the aromatic scent of the bayberry, and it was a reasonable substitute for the more desirable tea from across the water.

He had to admit, he was beginning to feel his age. He was tired. His once blond hair was turning white, making it appear lighter than ever. His shoulders were beginning to droop; and when he looked at his hands, he was reminded of his father's hands when he grew old. He was waiting for Jacob who had promised to stop by with news from town. Soon it would be time to tend the animals.

The Patch men like most all of the men in Groton and in the Massachusetts Bay Colony harbored growing resentment toward the British. Parliament had been attempting to impose taxes and levies on many goods shipped into and out of Boston in order to bolster the British treasury. New England settlers felt like second-class citizens with no ability to change conditions for the better. It just wasn't right. What are we to do, thought Ebenezer. It's a form of incarceration, I say. Resentment continued to boil about the

Stamp Act that Parliament had attempted to impose as well as to the group of acts that had become known as the Intolerable Acts. Things were getting worse not better, and Ebenezer worried for the safety of his family and for their future.

The sound of hoof beats signaled the arrival of Jacob who tethered his horse to the newly installed granite post by the front door and walked around to the kitchen where he knew Ebenezer would be waiting. He no sooner walked through the door when he began talking:

"Well, you will never guess what just happened. You remember that Reverend Dana wasn't allowed back into the meeting house the Sabbath after his awful sermon. Apparently there was formal talk about the situation between Reverend Dana and some of the deacons of the church, Doctor Prescott and a few others. What that means is that Reverend Dana will have to promise the town that he will not oppose them politically but will join with them on matters advised by the Continental and Provincial Congresses as well as on matters that the town has voted on. If he agrees to do that, then he'll be restored to his previous position in the town; but if he doesn't agree, then he can no longer be our pastor! Imagine that. He has been here about fifteen years, I do believe, and a Harvard man too. It sounds like a threat to me. Anyhow, Reverend Dana came to the meeting, said that he had thought about the matter and asked the town to dismiss him."

"Land's sake," interjected Ebenezer. "Now on top of everything else we don't have a pastor."

"That's right," Jacob chuckled, "And do you know what else? You remember how hard the wind blew on that Sunday when he gave that sermon. Some are calling that tirade the 'Windy Sermon' because, as you remember, one of the horse stables blew down while he was delivering that speech."

"You know, Jacob, this controversy has been going on now for a couple of months. It was back at the end of March when the church people met but refused to make any formal charges against the Reverend, and he refused to confess to anything wrong. After that, the church folks were not able to get the Reverend to set another meeting; they wrote him and talked with him, but he refused even though one written request was signed by the majority of the members of the church. By the end of May, I hear, we are going to have the Reverend Doctor Cooper from Boston preach." Ebenezer chuckled, "Now, Jacob, tell me what's going on in Boston."

"I don't know what's going on down there, Father. I did hear that more Redcoats are coming all the time, even more generals. Most everyone is still talking about the Reverend Dana situation. I don't know whether he and his family will stay in town or move on. As far as Boston goes, I think things are not going well. The Redcoats seem to be settling in. There are skirmishes with our lads every now and then."

"I did hear a rumor that some of our boys actually did fight at Concord on April 19th. Here's how they say it happened. According to Nathan Corey, on the day before the fight while he was plowing, he received notice of an urgent meeting of the Minutemen. It was late in the afternoon, near sun down. He left his oxen in the field, grabbed his musket and went on into town to join the others. Apparently the meeting was called because the cannon were coming. It was suggested by someone that the Minutemen should take a vote as to whether they should proceed straight away to Concord; but when it was taken, the vote didn't pass because they thought they should wait for more information.

"But several of them, nine in fact, including Nathan started for Concord that night! They apparently walked all night carrying lighted torches, reaching Concord early in the morning. They stopped for breakfast at Colonel Barrett's house, and after eating went into the center of town to join up with the Concord men. They ended up near the North Bridge. That's where the fighting occurred, you know. Corey and our boys continued with the Minutemen, following the retreating Redcoats into Lexington and beyond. Imagine!"

"Well, I'll be—", grunted Ebenezer, "Good for Nathan. Always knew that lad was worthy. But how do you suppose Nathan and the others knew that trouble was about to start. We're thirty miles from Boston!"

"I don't know, Father, but I suppose it might have something to do with the fact that the cannon appeared on the common all of a sudden. There is a bit more good news. Apparently on the tenth of this month the Second Continental Congress met in Philadelphia. That military man, George Washington, was there, and apparently the famous Ben Franklin has returned to America from London. That's important.

"There has been military activity over on the border with New York at Fort Ticonderoga. Some of our boys from Groton were there. Apparently the leaders felt that our colonies here in New England could be separated from the other colonies if the Redcoats came down from Canada by way of Lake Champlain, Lake George, the Hudson River and on to New York. That would cut us off. So, what did they do? They picked Ethan Allen; you've heard of him. He gathered up his Green Mountain Boys.

"At the same time the Massachusetts Committee of Safety asked Benedict Arnold to raise an army. Allen's men stormed the Fort where the gate was wide open and the British sentry was asleep! It was an easy victory, and our lads confiscated a significant amount of supplies, cannon balls and mortar that we can surely use. And, a couple of days later, we captured Crown Point not far away.

This is really exciting because our control of those areas means that we are now protected against an invasion down through Canada!"

"Now, you're giving me good news, Jacob. I have been so very worried, particularly after that confrontation in Concord. I have been fearful that we could not gain a victory. You best be moving along now. I know that you are busier than a moth in a mitten getting ready for your next commitment."

After Jacob left, Ebenezer finished his tea, put on his old felt hat and left the house to begin the evening chores. Black fly season was in full swing, and they were flitting and buzzing around Ebenezer's head as he walked to the barn. Not only is Jacob harried these days, he thought, but so are Benjamin and Simon, all trying to get things in order at home as they know more fighting lies ahead.

We must fight for the things we believe in what ever the cost. What price will we be required to pay for the rights and freedoms that all human beings deserve. Ebenezer's heavy thoughts lifted a bit as he entered the squeaky barn door and felt the radiating warmth of the animals who greeted him. He was comforted by the gentle, rhythmic sounds of cattle chewing and the sweet smells of last year's hay. A fleeting smile crossed his face as he marveled at his good fortune, thankful that at least for this particular moment in time all was well.

* * *

The Minutemen, already organized in numerous towns and ready to fight, promptly obeyed the summons to enlist in the growing army; and by the time the British had been driven from the North Bridge, all roads leading to Concord had been thronged by men hurrying to the scene of action. In most instances they carried the old flintlock musket that had fought the Indians, and the drum that beat at Louisburg. They were led by men who had served under General Wolfe at Quebec.

The tragic deaths of Amos Farnsworth's brother, Benjamin, and his father had shaken the town's people of Groton to the core. While crossing the Nashua River in a canoe, the previous December, they had both drowned when the canoe capsized. The brother's body was located shortly after the accident, and the funeral was held on December 11th. The body of his father was not discovered until March when it was found on the 10th between Longley's Island and Jacquith's Mill about a mile below the mill. A second funeral was held. It was an incredibly sad time for Amos.

Locally Thursday, May 9, 1776, was a day set apart by the town for fasting and prayer that "God be so pleased to send us a man for preacher that will be faithful over the flock." Reverend Mr. Whitney of Shirley preached in the morning and Reverend Mr. Emerson, in the afternoon of that day.

Friday, May 17th was a day set apart by the Grand Congress as a day of fasting and prayer throughout the land. These were difficult times for all.

Chapter X

BATTLE OF BUNKER HILL

The next month Artemas Ward, then forty eight years of age, was appointed General and Commander-in-Chief of all forces raised by Congress for the defense of the colony, but this commission did not necessarily authorize him to command the forces raised elsewhere. Men from other colonies were arriving daily at Cambridge.

Ward's task was to bring order to an army of men that had grown rapidly following the Battle of Lexington and Concord. All were volunteers. Many had fought in the French wars, and many more had served in militia companies. Each had left his farm or place of business with the idea of fighting the British and then quickly returning home. These men did not adapt readily to camp life. Food was scarce at first; and the comforts of home, lacking.

Ward in his earlier years was a teacher in Groton and married Sarah Trowbridge, daughter of the Groton minister with whom he boarded, and in the intervening years he developed a significant amount of experience. In 1763 he was commissioned as a colonel and regularly conducted training required at that time in all towns. He had urged his men to fight for the King against the French but later prepared them to resist the encroachments of George III. He earned fame and popularity, both militarily and in the civil affairs of the Colony. It was he who issued the order to move forces to Bunker Hill.

* * *

The next military engagement close to home occurred in June. Oliver was the only one of Ebenezer's sons who participated in that battle, and Groton and its neighboring towns were well represented by Colonel William Prescott's Regiment. On Friday, June 16, 1775, Prescott's troops were sent into the Charlestown Peninsula to occupy Bunker Hill. Believing Breed's Hill would be more advantageous, they instead occupied Breed's Hill. Breed's Hill was lower in height and closer to the enemy; in fact, it was within cannon range of the ships in the harbor.

The troops and their commanders worked deep into the night by starlight without food or sleep, constructing an earthen fortification or redoubt to protect the hill top. After its completion, General Putnam ordered the men to throw away their shovels and other tools by carrying them down the back of the hill. Those men estimated to be about 150 in number never came back to fight.

The next morning, Saturday, Colonel Prescott, refused relief for his remaining men saying, "The men who built this fort will best defend it." Early in the morning while mist still lay heavy over the harbor obscuring the activities of his men, two small cannon were brought to the redoubt. The remaining troops on the hill, about 163 strong, were forced to fortify the cannon with their bare hands as the tools had been removed earlier. Men never worked with more zeal. Many dug until their fingers bled. To loosen the earth a cannon was loaded and aimed to fire into the gap, and this was repeated once. However, missing their targets, both cannon balls fell in Boston itself, one near the meeting house on a square, and the other fell on Cornhill.

Later in the morning after the fog had lifted, the British were surprised to discover the progress made by the enemy during the night, and they responded with aggression. They could be seen from the hill about ten o'clock in the morning along with four or five men-of-war and several armed boats on the Mystic River. When the Redcoats first made their appearance around one o'clock, a portion of the men in the redoubt wavered and prepared to retreat; but both Colonel Prescott and Captain Bancroft addressed them, and from that time on the men stood up bravely to the task at hand.

During the afternoon of June 17th the British were under the leadership of General William Howe who led his force of 3,000 men ashore near the south side of Breed's Hill, making two assaults up the hill against the colonists. Colonel Prescott ordered his small band of patriots not to fire until they saw the "whites of the Redcoat's eyes," to aim low and to fire at the fine coats themselves. Every man took deadly aim.

The line of Redcoats approached as though on dress parade. Notwithstanding the orders, a half a dozen random shots were fired. Then a deadly volley fell upon the red line which wavered, fractured and fell back. Again the formation was reestablished, and again it was shattered. The advances of the Redcoats were thwarted, resulting in heavy losses to the British forces, and more troops were summoned.

A third time the British prepared to assault, and they moved forward as a body. This advance occurred when the Americans were running dangerously low on ammunition and were afraid of being flanked. The Redcoats were approaching on both sides. Captain Bancroft had already fired twenty seven rounds and had only one round left. Suddenly it seemed the Redcoats were in the redoubt. British bayonets lashed out at the Americans who threw rocks and used their muskets to protect themselves, lashing back at the Redcoats. An officer sprang from the parapet. Captain Bancroft fired at him, and then he himself fell. He cleared the redoubt as ball after ball whizzed by. One took off a forefinger. On Charlestown

Neck he met reinforcements under the command of Captain Samuel Gerrish. Bancroft was weak and exhausted from loss of blood. Seeing a tethered horse by the road, a soldier helped him onto it, and Bancroft made his way to safety.

Colonel Prescott was forced to retreat around sunset with his remaining forces down the north side of Breed's Hill, resulting in many more casualties during the retreat. Most of those killed were shot in the back as they scrambled down the hill, leaving the ground on both sides of the hill a mass of dead and dying bodies. When the American troops reached Cambridge later that night, that village of about 300 houses was nearly in ashes.

Oliver Patch was wounded in the shoulder, and he lost his musket in the battle for which his mother was later reimbursed.

Prudence Wright's brother Benjamin served in this battle where he lost his knapsack. He was only nineteen years of age.

Twelve soldiers from Groton were either wounded or killed that day, more than from any other town. Others were taken captive and later died.

Although this battle, known as the Battle at Bunker Hill, seemed not to advance the cause of liberty, the British learned that the Americans were willing to fight and to die for their cause. Later it became known that George Washington had been named commander-in-chief on June 15th and was on his way to Massachusetts when the fighting occurred. He assumed command on July 3rd under an elm tree in Cambridge and then devoted the next several months to organizing and to training his soldiers.

Chapter XI

FUTURE PLANS

Closer to home the days following those horrific events were days of profound change in Groton. The streets were nearly deserted of townspeople. However, there were caravans of travelers headed north to the more sparsely settled towns and remote settlements in New Hampshire. Some were searching for a place in the far away wilderness where they could hopefully camp in safety. Others were folks from the devastated towns north of Boston. Most were laden with personal belongings and sentimental treasures that they hoped to preserve. A few of the lucky traveled with carts, but many families were walking. Most groups were made up of old or crippled men, women of all ages and young children. Strong young and middle-aged men were rarely seen. Such was the aftermath of the British raid on Middlesex County.

On June 28, 1774, Oliver Prescott, as a member of Groton's Committee on Correspondence and in response to the Port Bill, wrote to the Overseers of the Poor in Boston indicating that forty bushels of grain, part rye and part Indian corn, had been sent for the welfare of Boston's poor, many of whom were now in the process of removing to various neighboring towns and relative safety.

The natives of Groton had neither fled in panic nor had they been driven from their homes but instead were laboring industriously, too focused and too worried to visit their neighbors or freely move about. Men and older boys were leaving almost daily to sign up in the burgeoning army, some for only a few days and others for the unknown duration of hostilities. Women were spinning and weaving clothing for the men folks in the Boston area, many of whom had enlisted without ever going home for wearables.

Other items needed by the military were shoes, boots, coats, shirts and blankets, meat and all other food stuffs. Groton could offer little in the way of armaments, but members of the village certainly would strive to provide all that they could. One strategic mistake made during this war was the establishment of short enlistment periods, sometimes only a few days in duration, making the task of creating a long-term army of predictable size extremely difficult.

Those citizens of Groton who were not in sympathy with the idea of separation from England, although few in number, were very, very quiet these days. They gave no reason to draw attention to themselves and expressed few opinions.

In the evenings carts would begin to appear on the roads, and the long arduous night trip to Cambridge would begin. Carts heavy with clothing, food and other necessities contributed by friends and neighbors would make up a full load, and the return from this perilous journey was anxiously awaited with great expectation.

Who did you see? How did he look? What did he say? Has he enough to eat and wear? What's going on in Boston? What do you think will happen next? This last question was indeed almost impossible to answer even for the leaders of the Bay Colony. The English army had become well entrenched in Boston. The future for those residents who, by choice or lack of opportunity, remained in the city was indeed bleak. Those unlucky folks could look forward to a lack of food and fuel if this stalemate were to continue for an extended period. No one was allowed to leave or enter the city without extensive examination and hard-to-get permission, virtual prisoners in their own town.

The volunteer army grew in size by the day. Where to camp and how to feed the men was becoming an increasingly serious challenge. Other colonies were sympathetic to the Bay Colony in spirit and for its losses suffered as well as for its occupation by militant invaders. Connecticut, for one, sent a fully uniformed and equipped company. Companies as well as meager, unsupervised groups and lone individuals wandered into camp.

Occasionally a few mountain men dressed in hunters' clothing came carrying unusually long barreled rifles, some said to be as long as its carrier was tall. These latter soldiers had no commander and wanted none. All they wanted was to get a shot at the invaders; they were self-sufficient individuals. Each carried a camp kettle, and he planned to find for himself something to cook in it.

Local volunteers spent time, not taken up by military drill, improvising rudimentary shelters of many creative types. Where nature provided a natural ledge of rock, it was not difficult for the ingenious to fashion some kind of functional roof. Boards from a partially burned building or fallen tree branches were used as thatch and were frequently seen. Fortunately, the weather was moderate in late spring, and many wanted no overhead shelter, needing only a large wool blanket.

* * *

Preparatory efforts were also underway at the homestead of Ebenezer Patch. After a family conference, it was decided that Benjamin would remain at home for a short time, possibly a few weeks, so that he and Ebenezer could finish the spring plowing and plant as much corn and potatoes as possible on every piece of available land. They would plant as much seed as Ebenezer and the children could care for, and then Benjamin would join Oliver in Cambridge.

Up in Ashby Simon and Elizabeth worked together from day break until dark so that if military conditions required, Simon would be able to join his brothers in Cambridge. Elizabeth finally accepted the inevitability of this most likely turn of events. Despite the lack of timely news, they could not imagine the colony turning back after the hostile confrontations at Concord and Boston and all the events preceding those battles. They could see nothing ahead but a very bitter, all-out contest.

Elizabeth fretted constantly about her brothers, three of whom had gone to battle. She planned to stay in Ashby on their homestead at all costs. Rebecca, the oldest child, could help some, and she, Elizabeth, needed to take time some sunny day to go down over the Throne to visit Aunt Elizabeth Lakin. Old as she was Aunt Elizabeth could take care of the house and the two younger children. She was a wise old lady who knew all about the hardships of earlier years in the settlement and how to manage in almost any situation. Simon and Elizabeth had worked tirelessly and productively since beginning their new life together up in Ashby, but now there was even greater urgency to achieve progress.

Jacob's preparatory planning was easier. His father, mother and younger siblings were just down at the foot of the hill. His wife's family was only a mile or so away. He felt reassured that everyone would be able to manage during his absence, and he had made up his mind that he would soon return to his company in Cambridge. He and Ebenezer were plowing and planting during as many daylight hours as possible.

Benjamin's situation was similar. He did not as yet have a wife or children, and he felt a deep obligation to his parents and to his brothers and sisters. Strong ties of dependency and caring bound the Patch family together. Both he and Jacob shared the notion that the fighting would remain in the colony and that somehow they could alternately come home for a few days at a time when military activity allowed. Oliver rejected that idea and was determined to stay at the center of activity until the Redcoats were driven far out into the sea.

By June the planting was complete. The Patch men could breath a sign of relief as their immediate short-term goals had been met. They planted all the seed held over from fall. Stored in cloth wraps, it came out of storage, one bag at a time and was amply sown into rows on the freshly plowed fields. Oddly, there had been little rain since the spring rains ceased back in early April, it was, and barely a drop had fallen since.

On June 20th the Groton survivors of the battle at Breed's Hill arrived home by way of Lincoln.

Chapter XII

SUMMER 1775

Summer slowly followed on the heels of spring as it always does, and George Washington arrived in Massachusetts early in July. He was revered in Virginia following the French Wars more than twenty years earlier when he had served with the British, but he had no recent military experience. It was with some reluctance that he came out of military retirement and away from the comfort of his plantation to become military commander for all of the colonies. Washington's experience was limited to that of participating with the British army and as commander of the Virginia forces. In his early military life he had aspired to become a commissioned officer of the British army.

However, in later years his view of England changed through his experiences as a tobacco farmer. He came to realize how unfairly he and other farmers were being treated by the British. They sold tobacco and other crops to the British at rock-bottom prices and yet were forced to purchase supplies and other imported goods at inflated prices. By the time of the Revolution, Washington had become a strong supporter of American independence.

Upon reaching Boston, he quickly found that the Bay Colony's army was a rebellious, undisciplined lot. Many of its members were farmers who had neither participated in periodic drills nor had belonged to any organized militia. Others were Minutemen who had participated in drills but were poorly organized. All were inadequately clothed by Washington's standards. One could not determine who was in charge as there were no uniforms. Those who wore tri-cornered hats could have been either officers, medical personnel or chaplains; one could not be sure. Most wore home-spun clothing. There was no organized shelter. Drinking of rum and other spirits was commonplace. Cleanliness of clothes and body was impossible to maintain as the troops spent considerable time working the earth to construct defense lines, and they had no way of cleaning themselves even if they had so desired. Illness increased as time went on. However, the troops were well fed as fresh produce was still being delivered by cart from the surrounding towns. There was neither an accurate count as to numbers of troops nor a reliable estimate of the numbers of British.

In addition, Washington did not know the terrain. During his participation with the British he became very familiar with the country side west of Virginia as he had surveyed those lands in earlier years. Here he was totally unfamiliar with the complexities of Boston's waterfront, harbors, inlets, swamps and hills. He quickly became aware that the American troops were entrenched in an arc on the high land around the town of Boston and that the British were holed up in the town itself with their ships anchored off the coast and their guns aimed on shore. An omnipotent fear of attack by the British permeated the American forces night and day. It was not until several weeks later that Washington learned of the pitifully low quantity of ammunition on hand, a mere nine rounds per man. Money was scarce, and he needed spies.

* * *

The summer of 1775 proved to be unseasonably hot and dry, much more so than at any other time within recent memory. The Patch men began to fret as it soon became evident that the newly planted seeds were not germinating as they normally did. The lack of rain was being felt. By the end of June the soil was beginning to resemble fine brown-gray powder. Cracks began to appear in the corn fields, particularly those on higher elevations. By July the growth of corn was sparse, and the plants were stunted in size. Corn ears were only partially filled with kernels. Fields of corn planted on lower elevations or those that received partial shade seemed healthier.

Ebenezer Patch surveyed his fields with dismay, and he knew that his concerns were shared by Jacob and Simon. Despite dry conditions, Ebenezer and Benjamin went through the motions of hoeing the corn rows to prevent excessive weed growth; and because of the extreme heat, they preferred to engage in this activity early in the morning before the sun rose high in the sky. Sometimes Jacob joined them, and always Benjamin's best friend, George, would be near at hand with his nose to the ground sniffing out the latest trail of a field mouse or an even larger critter if he could find one. The three Patch men could often be found together, sharing stories of the day while engaged productively. Each man would work a row, and as they toiled side by side, they talked.

"Jacob, I know you keep your ear to the ground and go into town often. Bring us up to date", proffered Ebenezer as he leaned against the handle of his hoe, taking off his hat to wipe the sweat from his brow.

"Well, Father, there's talk about price controls. I don't know if it will happen, but the General Assembly is apparently considering an act which would divide the state into districts with a committee chosen for each district to fix the price of labor and provisions."

Benjamin, looking puzzled, asked, "Jacob, why would they do that? What would that do?"

"As you know, with everyone in the army, there is no one left to work the farms or provide services in town. So those who are not in the army can demand higher wages. The problem is that there is no money to pay them. No one has any money. We are sending provisions in to Cambridge for the militia, and no one is getting paid for them. We know that crops will be poor this year because it's so dry; that will make matters worse for everyone. And just think about how valuable your oxen have become!" Price controls were in fact enacted, but they were abolished after a short period of time.

"I can attest to that," offered Ebenezer woefully, "Why, just look at this place. Our crops are likely to be down by half at least. It's the same up on your place, too, Jacob, and I'm sure Simon is not faring any better than we are." Ebenezer's mind wandered off for a moment as he thought about how much he prized his own New Hampshire yellow oxen. They would, of course, be even more valuable to the army, he thought, as they are wonderful working animals. I hope the army doesn't need them! Why, they are even more valuable than a horse. The only thing a horse is good for is for faster travel.

"There's talk that it will be hard to pay the men in Cambridge because of the shortage of money. That's not a good thing. The enlistment periods are short, and it will be hard to get the men to reenlist if they are not paid for the current enlistment."

"Well, I'll be——," muttered Ebenezer.

"Folks are still talking about the fighting at the North Bridge and at Breed's Hill. They say that Colonel William Prescott was the commander of our men at Breed's Hill and that he could have won that battle if only he had had more ammunition. You know he was born here in Groton even though he lives in Pepperell now. A lot of our boys died there that day, but the British lost even more. After the Colonel returned to Cambridge, he volunteered to go back to the Hill and try to retake it if they would give him three regiments of men and sufficient ammunition or die in trying, so they say, but it didn't happen."

"Too bad," grunted Benjamin in understanding, "We might have been able to end this thing right then and there!"

"According to the grape vine telegraph," began Benjamin, using a phrase he had heard to describe how news traveled, "Major John Pitcairn was shot by a black man from Groton while he was rallying the British troops who had dispersed. Shot him right through the head, he did. 'Course he died later, you know."

"S'that so!"

The men worked in silence for a few minutes, each deep in thought, but methodically loosening brittle, taupe soil around parched plants of undersized corn to discourage encroaching weed growth. George trotted by every now and then just to let them know he was still with them.

"Jacob, have you heard anything from Simon and Elizabeth? I know several of Elizabeth's brothers were at Breed's."

"Yes, that's right. The Williams family has suffered unmercifully. I think Elizabeth is still grieving over her father's death, and her mother is up there on the farm all alone. Elizabeth's brother, Daniel, came back from Cambridge about the time you did, Ben. Jacob Williams marched when we did on April 19th to Cambridge. He enlisted on the 25th for ninty eight days. They expect him back around the first of August. The family thinks that he was at the battle on Breed's Hill, but they're not sure. Jason, you remember, marched when we did. He came back a few days before we did but plans to go back in the fall."

"Oh, I almost forget to tell you about Reverend Dana. They say that he wrote a letter of apology to the town. You remember a while back when someone shot bullets into his house. No one hurt, though, fortunately. More recently, I think on the 26th of last month, June it was, a couple of fellows down from Mason, New Hampshire, went into Dana's pasture, they did, took a three-year-old red heifer and killed it. Then they used it for themselves. Took the meat home, I suppose. Then they took off and joined up with our lads in Cambridge. Guess they just don't abide them Tories."

The letter requesting forgiveness signed by Samuel Dana was dated May 23, 1775, and stated in part, ". . .do hereby sincerely ask Forgiveness of all such for whatever I have said or done, that had the least Tendency to the Injury of my Country, assuring them that it is in full Purpose, in my proper sphere, to unite with them in all those laudable and fit measures, that have been recommended by the Continental and Provincial Congresses. . ." Reverend Dana remained in Groton for a few years preaching to the Presbyterian Society before moving away.

Jacob continued, "I also heard that one of Colonel Prescott 's sisters was married to a Loyalist. She's dead now, Elizabeth Prescott, I mean, and her husband Abijah Willard married twice more. Anyhow, Abijah accepted the position of Mandamus Counselor a few months ago but was forced to give it up by a mob of our boys in Connecticut somewhere, Stafford, I think. Anyhow, they took him up to Sturbridge. Then Willard went into Boston on April 19th and became a commissary in the British army!"

"Hard to know who to trust anymore," muttered Ebenezer.

"Who were the fellows who killed the heifer, do you know?" asked Ben.

"I think they said it was Jason Russell and John Tarbell. I wonder if they are related to the Groton Tarbell's," replied Jacob.

Each town was responsible for determining who was a Loyalist, and those individuals so identified were often relieved of their arms, ammunition and any other weapons in their possession. They were also confined to their farms or at least could not leave the town limits. Often they were jailed at the discretion of the town, and those accused could not appeal the decision. Emotions ran high; and loyalties, strong.

"Sun's up, boys," offered Ebenezer. "Must be neigh onto nine o'clock. Someone will be bringing us baiting soon." The Revolutionary breakfast consisted of bread and milk. At about nine o'clock lunch or baiting was customarily brought out to the field with a bottle of cider. No sooner had Ebenezer spoken when the slam of a door could be heard echoing in the distance, and little Ruthie could be seen running through the yard with a basket, her skirts ballooning out behind her as she ran. Soon she would be in the corn field and out of sight among the rows.

"Here she comes now. Let's go out to the end of the row where she can find us easy and find a tree and some shade along the fence." Benjamin and Jacob didn't need another invitation. They quickly dropped their tools and headed for shade.

Chapter XIII

Samuel

Crops of corn and potatoes were pitifully small in the summer of 1775. Some plantings failed completely. The hay harvest was half of what would normally have been expected. The Patch men as a group bemoaned the sparse crops and worried collectively about the adequacy of food for the winter for both man and beast. It would be far from a bumper year. Even the apples and peaches were runted in size and fewer than usual.

It was too hot to work. On some mornings the suffocating humidity felt like a wet blanket covering everything. It was insufferably oppressive, but it did not rain. Occasionally a few token drops fell, but it was so hot that the rain dried up before reaching the thirsty, sere ground. Many days of steady rain would be needed to restore the parched earth, but it was already too late for this year's harvest. Everyone was grouchy and cross. By five o'clock it was all Ebenezer could do to get himself up out of the chair after eating a light evening meal to go and care for the animals. He wasn't feeling well at all. Perhaps it's just the heat, he thought. I'll feel better in the fall when the weather changes.

But conditions would become much worse before they improved. Illness was pervasive throughout the town, and the death rate was much higher than usual. It was some kind of unexplained fever, people speculated. Soldiers were deserting; they were bored and tired of drills. They had lost their zeal. Others came home when their enlistments were over. Food shortages were beginning to occur. Sickness continued to increase everywhere. Soldiers coming home from camp brought dysentery and fever with them.

Little news was forthcoming now from Boston. Everyone hoped that General Washington and the new army would somehow force the British out to sea and banish them back to England without ado. Even Jacob, Benjamin and Simon were becoming complacent, believing that they might not have to leave home again. Occasionally a story would be heard about some local fellow or some perceived movement in the military mission. Still the British continued to occupy Boston. On August 24th a four-year-old child of Mr. John Bowers drowned by falling into a vat in his tan yard.

It was on an evening late in August as Sarah was tucking little Samuel into bed when he complained, "Mama, I don't feel good."

"What's the matter, Sam, do you hurt?"

"No, nothing hurts. I just feel draggy."

"Draggy? You mean tired?"

"Yes, that's it, tired."

"Well, maybe after a good night's sleep, you'll feel better. Let's wait until tomorrow and see how you feel then."

The next morning after a restless night Sam seemed a bit worse. "Now I'm draggy and hot," he complained, "And my head hurts."

"Just stay quiet today, and perhaps it will pass,"

During the next few days Samuel, having just passed his tenth birthday stayed home and in the house. He felt fairly well in the morning; but as the day wore on he felt worse and by late afternoon, he was again feverish. Each morning Sarah heated water in one of her fireplace kettles, placed some of his clothes in it and then wrapped his wrists with the hot cloth, placing more at the back of his neck. As a precautionary measure she gave him hot milk to which a few drops of iodine had been added to prevent the onset of a miserable cold. After five days Samuel felt no better, and he began to feel what he described as a "flutter."

Then came the day around the 3rd of September when Ebenezer made a decision. It's time to get Doctor Oliver Prescott, he thought, and he bade Benjamin to saddle one of the horses, go into town and find the good doctor.

Doctor Prescott, then forty four years of age, had young children of his own, so that when a citizen of Groton called upon his services to care for a child, he gave it his top priority. A graduate of Harvard College, he had studied medicine under Doctor Robey of East Sudbury and had developed an extensive practice in his home town of Groton as well as fulfilling his many civic responsibilities. It was said of him that his demeanor displayed a reserved politeness and a meticulous attention to detail. He was loved and respected by all.

Sarah and Ebenezer were sitting at the kitchen table when they heard the pounding sound of double hoof beats approaching rapidly, stampeding to a stop near the front door. That would be Benjamin and Doctor Prescott, thought Ebenezer. Thank goodness, he's arrived! Doctor Prescott's tall shadow loomed large in the open doorway. He was accompanied by Benjamin's friend, George. He stepped through the mud room into the kitchen, and Benjamin, having successfully accomplished his mission, unsaddled his sweaty, wheezing horse, cooled him down as best he could and led him to pasture.

"Hello, Ebenezer. Sarah. I hear you have some sickness here with your boy. What seems to be the matter?"

"I don't know, doctor. Sam's been sick near a week now and not getting any better. I've tried everything I know to help him. Hot compresses. Iodine milk. I don't know what else to do." Sarah offered nearly in tears, "We're really getting scared. We've already lost four children, and with four more going off to fight. . .," her voice trailed off, "I'm too old to have any more."

"There, there, my dear. Just let me take a look at him." Doctor Prescott found Samuel lying on a temporary pallet on the floor in the front parlor. As he knelt down, he knew immediately that little Sam was indeed sick. Not just a cold, I fear, he thought. Sam's skin felt hot and clammy. His pulse was rapid. "How are you feeling today, Sam?"

"I feel dreamy, kind of out of myself," he responded weakly.

"I understand, son." Doctor Prescott did not move for several moments. He was mulling over in his mind how to tell this distraught mother and worried father that their beautiful small son could be seriously ill. Slowly, he arose from the floor and returned to the kitchen. As he sat in one of the kitchen chairs, he lowered his voice so that he would not be heard by Sam.

"I'm afraid this could be serious, Sarah. . . Ebenezer. His heart rate is higher than it should be. He is feverish. Perhaps some kind of inflammation. Could be the fever. There's a lot of it going around. Soldiers bringing it back from the camp in Cambridge. Has he been in town lately?" he asked, not waiting for a reply, "With your permission, I would like to bleed him. If we take off a bit of blood, it may lower his heart rate and help his fever. Keep on with the compresses. I'm going to leave some medicine with you before I leave." Doctor Prescott groped around in his bag for a lancet, and finding one rose to go back into the front room and perform the procedure.

Sarah sat at the table, hands covering her face, sobbing quietly. Ebenezer rose from his chair, went down on his knees at her side and took her in his arms. He buried his face in her neck while slowly stroking her disheveled hair. Without saying a word, each knew what the other was thinking. What are we to do. Our first

Samuel died when he was only three. We can't lose another one. From the other room they could hear a low scream, and they knew that the lancet had been placed in Samuel's little arm. "Oh, my god," Sarah lamented, "I can't bear any more!"

Doctor Prescott's expression was somber when he returned to the kitchen and packed up his bag. "That's all we can do for now. I hope I don't have to bleed him again. When his heart rate comes down, his tongue will likely be dry, and he may become delirious. I'll give you some mercury for the fever, and I'm going to leave you with some tincture of quinine. It might help. I'll write out the instructions. Make sure he gets plenty of fresh air while the weather is warm; and if he will eat, give him wholesome food. Try some bark water; you know how to do that, Sarah. Just heat some water and place the bark in it to steep; then give him as much of the water as he will take. Keep the other children away from him. I think I know how you must be feeling, my dear. I know how I would feel if he were one of mine. I'll stop by in a couple of days, but if you need me in the meantime, just send Benjamin for me."

"We will, doctor, thank you," Ebenezer murmured as he went to the door with the doctor. Turning back to the kitchen, "Sarah, perhaps Benjamin should go up to Jacob's and have Mary come down to help you take care of Sam. We can all take turns staying up with him. Maybe her mother (Betty Nutting Hazen) can come down to take care of Jacob's children until Sam improves. Bette's children are all grown. Her husband (Benjamin) has passed, and she is on her place by herself. And so it happened that Mary Hazen Patch became a part of Ebenezer's household for the next few days.

By September 7th young Samuel Patch was not improved despite the efforts of his mother and sister-in-law. In fact, his condition had deteriorated dramatically. His tongue was still dry and was now crusting; he was unable to eat or drink. He was delirious off and on. His skin was developing blisters and was peeling from his body. Doctor Prescott had made several visits, and on today's visit told Sarah that there was little else he could do. He left opium with instructions to give it to Samuel whenever he became extremely restless.

Two days later young Samuel Patch died, still lying on the temporary bedding in the front room in the company of his mother and Mary Hazen Patch. His tiny, emaciated body appeared blistered, and he had lost some hair. But now he lay white and still and cold, at peace at last, the sunny disposition of that happy little boy gone forever. Both women sat on the floor beside him crying, Sarah stroking his forehead and reliving all the sorrow and other emotions she had felt when her other small children had died.

Mary, never having lost a child, was in a state of shock, horrified by the enormity of it all and numbed by the experience. Why did little children have to suffer this way, she pondered. Why did anyone have to go through what Samuel had experienced. After what seemed like an interminable period of time, Sarah closed Samuel's eyes and wrapped his body in his blanket. Too tired to scream or wail, she was drained of strength and emotion. She would wash the body later and prepare it for burial.

Ebenezer knew when he left the house that morning at sun up that he and Benjamin would be constructing a pine casket before day's end. That is what they were doing when Sarah found them in the barn to tell them about Samuel. Ebenezer didn't say a word, but tears overflowed his pale blue eyes, streaming down his lined cheeks onto his well-worn shirt, now soaked with both sweat and tears. Benjamin put his arms around both parents, trying to comfort them as best he could.

* * *

Because of the war effort, the practice regarding funerals was changed in 1774 by the Continental Congress meeting then in Philadelphia thus, "On the death of any relation or friend none of us, or any of our friends, will go into any further mourning dress, than a black crepe or ribbon on the arm or hat, for gentlemen, and black ribbon and necklace for ladies, and we discontinue the giving of gloves and scarfs at funerals."

During the next few days, the family prepared for the funeral. While Ruthie and Ede were in school, Sarah and Ebenezer together washed Samuel's body and dressed it in his Sunday clothes. Meanwhile Benjamin lovingly completed the casket using the hand-hewn oak boards that he and Ebenezer had been working on the day Samuel died. After Mary returned home, Jacob rode up to Ashby to tell Simon and Elizabeth. Very quickly the Patch's extended family and neighbors learned of this untimely and unwelcome death.

Samuel's body was lowered into the lovingly prepared casket and was placed on a table in the front parlor so it could be viewed by everyone who came to call. People brought freshly baked bread, fruit preserves, anything close at hand that might help ease the pain of the Patch family. Along with these simple gifts they tried to bring comfort and solace to the grieving parents.

When the day of the funeral came, those same relatives and neighbors walked solemnly behind the pair of oxen and the cart carrying the remains of little Samuel Patch to its final resting place in Groton's Burying Ground beside the bodies of his brothers and sister who had gone before. A graveside service was performed by Reverend Daniel Chaplin, an imposing figure over six feet tall, who, along with Mr. Bigelow, had preached at the meeting house after the departure of Reverend Dana. It would not be until December 1776 that Mr. Chaplin would be ordained as pastor.

The days following Samuel's funeral were unspeakably miserable. Sarah and Ebenezer blindly and automatically went about their daily chores in silence, each lost in his own thoughts. Fall was rapidly approaching. There was much work to be done. By the first of September, the miserly hay crop had been stored in the barn. Puny ears of corn had been picked, and the brown, brittle corn husks had been chopped to the ground to be plowed under the following spring. Now, in mid-September it was time to finish gathering this year's undersized peaches, and soon it would be time to begin picking the meager apple crop. We need to harvest every bit of food on this farm, opined Ebenezer dismally.

Children would soon be gathering hickory nuts. Ebenezer's younger children were in school now where they were learning reading and writing. Little Ebenezer, the youngest child now two years of age, was the only child at home now during the day.

Then the unthinkable happened. One day baby Ebenezer became ill. His symptoms were similar to those experienced earlier by Samuel. He was hot and feverish. He cried constantly. Sarah still exhausted from the demands on her body from Samuel's illness looked drained and sallow. Clothes hung loosely about her tiny body. With the left over medicine Doctor Prescott had left for Samuel, she tried to help Ebenezer with compresses, iodine milk, bark water, quinine and finally opium. With Ebenezer's small body, progression of the disease was much more rapid than it had been with Samuel, and Doctor Prescott was not called. On the 30th of September Ebenezer died his mother's arms. Because a doctor had not been in attendance, Isaac Farnsworth, the newly appointed coroner was called.

This time, there were no tears. There were no tears left, only the undeniable sadness that accompanies fading dreams and deep sorrow. Sarah and Ebenezer with Benjamin's help went through the motions of preparing for the of burial and funeral, not believing that their second son named Ebenezer was also now gone. A phrase recalled from a recent sermon sprang to mind, "Upon what a slender thread do our lives hang on." Death was never easy.

Chapter XIV

ARTILLERY

In Boston British troops under the leadership of General William Howe continued to be confined to the city, surrounded by American militia, mostly from Massachusetts, Connecticut and New Hampshire, that now had become known collectively as the Continental Army. Arriving in Boston in 1715, Howe was considered by some to be sympathetic to the colonists. Nonetheless, he became temporary Commander of the British Army and later Commander-in-Chief.

Meanwhile, George Washington continued his attempts to coalesce his diverse troops into functioning units and to plan strategy. He had already learned a valuable lesson. The highly trained British were most effective and deadly when they could fight out in the open and in formation. American troops, on the other hand, were better at sniping in wooded areas and at surprise attacks.

The Continental Army continued to construct defenses on the hills surrounding the city of Boston, using the earth to build higher and higher protective fortifications. Once the ground became frozen such construction could no longer take place; and as cold weather came on, the troops would be idle. Lack of food, clothing, ammunition and money continued to be problematic. It would be a long, miserable winter. Desertions continued.

In December 1775 young Henry Knox, barely 25 years of age, was appointed Colonel of the Regiment of Artillery in a general order from the Continental Army Headquarters near Boston. He had been commissioned as a colonel on November 17th, and it was during November that the plan to siege Boston was developed. Born in Boston, Knox was largely self-educated, particularly in his area of interest which was military affairs, and he had served under Artemus Ward at Breed's Hill. As part of the plan it was decided that Knox would travel to Fort Ticonderoga and bring back the arms and ammunition stored there. The fort had been captured earlier by Benedict Arnold and Ethan Allen's Green Mountain Boys.

In the middle of November Henry Knox set out on horseback with his young 19-year-old brother, William. After the first day of travel, they reached Marlboro. Knox in a letter to his wife wrote that he had been caught in the "most violent northeast storm" he had ever seen. They traveled relatively uneventfully from Worcester to New York City, arriving there on November 25. During the two days they remained there, they made arrangements to send military supplies back to Boston. Traveling forty miles a day after leaving New York on December 1, they arrived in Albany where they also remained for a couple of days.

Bitter and unrelenting, penetrating cold characterized the day before they reached Fort Ticonderoga, and they spent the night at Fort George, traveling nearly eight hours the next day to reach the landing place at Ticonderoga on December 5th. Knox fortunately possessed a hardly nature, and this characteristic served him well. The next day was spent inspecting the artillery. Most pieces were too worn or too old to be of any use to the newly formed army. They then loaded what could be used onto a gondola, a flat boat that would transport the armaments over water. Usable pieces ranged from small mortar, guns ranging in size from four pounds to twenty four pounds, howitzers and larger mortar. Artillery pieces ranged from one foot to eleven feet in length and from 100 to 5,500 pounds in weight. Altogether the guns weighted

119,900 pounds, an unbelievable amount of weight to be carried nearly 300 miles by animal power in unpredictable winter weather over inhospitable terrain.

In addition to the cannon, there was one barrel of flints, considered the best in the country, along with Indian arrowheads and twenty three boxes of lead. The inventory of Henry Knox lists fifty nine pieces of hardware. Knox had previously arranged for the use of a scow and two other vessels, two-masted light, shallow craft or bateaux, for water transportation down Lake George. Fortunately, the lake had not completely frozen over although ice had already formed along both its sides.

By December 9th the guns had been laboriously loaded with tremendous difficulty, and the boats were pushed off across the surface of this picturesque lake. Knox left his young brother, William, in charge of the boats, a crew of soldiers and the hired civilians while the Colonel went ahead in the lighter craft.

Once on shore at the south end of the lake, Knox went about locating oxen, horses and sleds. Meanwhile William's scow ran aground on a hidden rock on the lake. After the scow was freed from its mooring on the rock, the unpredictable winds died down making the sails virtually useless. On Saturday Knox wrote, "We with difficulty reached Sabbath Day Point about nine in the evening. Went ashore and warmed ourselves by an exceeding good fire in a hut made by some civil Indians. They gave us some venison, roasted after their manner, which was very relishing."

The next day after several hours of much needed sleep, the group headed out again, but after only half an hour the wind sprang up against their sails, and for four hours they rowed as hard as they could, making little progress. On that day William's scow nearly sank, but the crew was able to bail out the water and continue on.

Exhausted again, they were forced ashore. They rested for several hours in the freezing cold beside a roaring fire.

The next day was just as difficult, but after six hours struggling again against the wind, they finally reached Fort George. They had traveled thirty three miles over the lake under the worse conditions imaginable. Here Knox planned the overland part of the trip. Heavy mortar and cannon were to go first. Each horse was to pull a specific amount of weight and no more. He sent a message to Squire Palmer at Stillwater asking him to amass the sleds and oxen and to be prepared to haul the cannon by the time of the first snow fall.

General Philip Schuyler arrived in Albany on December 7th to make arrangements for the ground part of this critical and adventure-filled trip. Fresh men and horses would be needed to navigate the mountains. Colonel Knox had sent letters to the Committees of Safety along the proposed route asking for food and shelter to be made available for both men and animals. So much could go wrong. They would likely need frequent replacements for horses, oxen and sleds.

Knox reported to Washington, "It is not easy to conceive of the difficulties we have had in getting the cannon over the lake, owing to the advanced season of the year and contrary winds. Three days ago, it was very uncertain whether we should have gotten them until next spring; but now, please God, they must go. I have made eighty two exceeding strong sleds and have provided eighty yoke of oxen to drag them as far as Springfield, where I shall get fresh cattle to carry them to camp. . .I hope in sixteen or seventeen days to be able to present to your Excellency, a noble train of artillery." It actually took forty days to traverse the nearly impassable route to the camp at Cambridge.

The men were forced to use horses in place of some of the oxen, requiring negotiation with the local folks who wanted more money for the use of their horses than Knox was authorized to spend. Finally the convey was underway and reached Glens Falls without additional noted incident. This odd-looking caravan represented virtually all of the artillery of the American Continental Army. Knox rode ahead with his advance party to be sure the trail was clear and to make advance preparations.

On Christmas eve, December 24th, snow finally fell, making it next to impossible for the horses to travel the eight miles beyond Saratoga where they would spend the night. On Christmas day they attempted to travel through snow more than two feet deep. After traveling only two miles they were forced to exchange their sleigh for saddle horses, and they finally arrived in Lansingburg, nine miles above Albany.

The next day travel was so treacherous that the horses refused to budge; they had to be left behind. The men were in Knox's words, "obliged to undertake a very fatiguing march of about two miles in snow three feet deep through the woods, there being no beaten path." Later they were loaned other horses, and they reached Albany in the afternoon as he wrote, "almost perished with cold." The guns had been temporarily abandoned back along the icy trail.

Knox spent the next four days with General Schuyler planning for replacements for men, horses, oxen and sleds. The soldiers from Ticonderoga and the civilians already hired were not sufficient to get the guns all the way back to Boston. Schuyler sent out his wagon master to scour the surrounding countryside, asking the residents to send in sleighs and horses at once. By December 31st 124 pairs of horses with sleighs had been located and placed into service.

On New Years Day Knox and his men cut holes in the ice at different crossings of the Hudson River in order to strengthen the ice by flooding it and allowing it to freeze again in order to support the weight of artillery and animals. Knox wrote, "a cruel thaw hinders from crossing the Hudson River." As the caravan finally passed through Albany, folks turned out to watch the awesome parade of metal, men and animals and turned out to help them cross the river. Schuyler reported that the arrival of the guns in Albany had been delayed by weak ice and mild weather. Again more sleighs and horses were procured, and again Knox headed out. At first the men traveled in groups, the largest one consisting of fourteen sleds, but after a few days they decided to remain closer together in order to help one another should the need arise.

On January 10th Knox entered the Berkshire Mountain area over hazardous terrain that led into a twelve-mile stretch known as Greenwoods, a dense, forbidding evergreen forest. From this point to East Otis there was much shouting and cracking of whips as the sled drivers pushed their animals to go on. They passed through the two Spectacle Ponds and then through a mountain pass where no road existed at all.

This was the most difficult leg of the entire trip, passing over mountains and along sharp precipices, chasms and deep valleys interspersed with rivers, lakes and dank swamps. Knox wrote, "It seemed almost a miracle that people with heavy loads should be able to get up and down such hills as are here." They used chains and poles under the sled runners and ropes anchored to trees to hold back the sleds or propel them forward whenever necessary.

When the caravan finally emerged from the dense mountain forest, it took what was once an Indian trail eastward. This trail in earlier days had provided ready communication between the

Indians of the Hudson and Connecticut River valleys. This trail, as was the Indian custom, did not follow the easier lower route in the valley but rather went up and down hills in as straight a line as possible, rounding only ponds, streams and swamps. There were no houses along the route from Albany to Springfield for over forty miles.

A receipt from a local man dated at Blandford, January 13, 1776, "Received of Henry Knox, eighteen shillings of lawful money for carrying a cannon weighing 243 pounds from this town to Westfield, being eleven miles".

When the caravan reached Westfield, the entire town came out. Most residents had never seen a cannon, much less big ones traveling over drifted snow. They traveled more slowly now as snow was melting in places and the ground, thawing in others. In Springfield fresh oxen were again obtained, and the New York men were released to return home.

By January 25th the ground was frozen again, and the caravan moved on to Framingham, where John Adams noted in his diary, "Thursday about 10 a.m. Mr. (Elbridge) Gerry called for me and we rode to Framingham where we dined. Colonel Buckminster, after dinner, showed us the train of artillery brought down from Ticonderoga by Colonel Knox."

The balance of this historic journey by Colonel Knox and his crew was relatively uneventful compared with the earlier hardships experienced by this small band of brave, robust men. The occupation of Boston and the strategy of General Washington in the early days of the Revolution depended upon the success of this mission. The expedition was expected to cost $1,000; its actual cost was $2,500, but as General Washington said, "The want of cannon is so great that no trouble or expense must be spared to get them," and it wasn't.

Henry Knox became a colorful character in his time, participating with the army throughout most of the active war and in many of its more famous battles. He was later promoted to major general and after the war was appointed to the office of Secretary of War. He remained in government for several more years, ultimately returning to his home in Maine where he engaged in farming and a wide array of business ventures, both worthy and nefarious. His risk-taking style remained a part of his persona for the rest of his life, but he died penniless and debt-ridden. Yet history will remember him for this single episode.

Chapter XV

WINTER 1775

Thanksgiving was late that year. In 1775 autumn thanksgivings had been ordered as usual in Connecticut and New Hampshire. Little was to be expected from the governor of Massachusetts in this time of turmoil, so the Provincial Congress meeting at Cambridge on October 22 issued a proclamation for a day of thanks signed "by order of the Provincial Congress, John Hancock, President," to be observed on December 15th.

Thanksgiving had always been a day of celebration, giving thanks to the Almighty for an abundant harvest; and after the customary church service a spectacular feast was enjoyed.

* * *

Oliver had come home during the early part of October from his second tour of duty. The wound he received at Breed's Hill was now completely healed, and he was courting Miss Alethea Blood. They hoped to be married in about two years after he had saved more money from his army enlistments. At the end of October he ordered a bounty coat or its equivalent in money. Either way, that would help. He and Alethea would be spending the day with Ebenezer and his family.

Benjamin, of course, would be at home, bringing with him for the feast his intended, Miss Persis Lewis, whom he also planned to marry as soon as he had enough money. Jacob and Mary would be there with Jacob Jr. Simon and Elizabeth would be spending the early part of the day with Elizabeth's mother and would come down with their three children to Ebenezer's later in the day.

However, this year would be different. Sarah Patch had closed the door to the room upstairs that been shared by Samuel and little Ebenezer and had no plans to ever open it again. Jacob and Mary's second child and first girl died on November 2, not quite one year old, and they were still mourning the loss. Yet this was a time for rejoicing and for sharing solemn thoughts as well.

* * *

On this day the large kitchen was teeming with excitement as Sarah, Mary, Alethea and Persis with the assistance of Ruthie and Ede were busy preparing the bountiful meal and setting tables with plates and mugs for hot spiced cider. One small table was set aside for the younger children, and the large pine table would be used by the grown folks.

Savory meat slowly roasting on both fireplace spits sent fat droplets sizzling into the dripping pan below. Venison, wild turkey and partridge were also favorites. There would be vegetables harvested earlier in the fall and stored in the cellar. In a large iron pot was squash, boiled and whipped, and in the warming pan were potatoes already roasted and warm baked apples. There would be pickles and a variety of preserves prepared earlier as the native berries had ripened. And, of course, butter, cheese and Sarah's famous corn pudding. The aromatic musty scent of baking bread emanated from the dutch oven, spreading throughout the entire first floor.

Mary brought with her several handsome peach and apple pies of various kinds that were warming in the oven. Benjamin and Oliver concentrated on a game of checkers at one end of the kitchen while

Ebenezer sat by the fire with George lying quietly at his feet, both waiting for the signal that it was time to eat.

As was the custom, Ebenezer gave thanks for the harvest, though not as bountiful as in past years, and for all the blessings bestowed upon this family, the fortitude to endure the heartaches it had suffered, for this comfortable home, for the land, for the livestock and for the ability of this family to sustain itself during times of adversity. He offered prayers to the Almighty for the continued safety of all its members, pray to God.

With the air still rich with excitement, everyone began to eat. It would be a long meal. Everyone was talking so loudly that conversations could barely be heard at first, and all the while children and adults alike were beginning to savor and appreciate the wide range of flavors and textures, the blend of scents and warmth from the roaring open fire.

Enjoying the moment, Benjamin offered, "You were right, Father, what you said last spring, about this place being able to take care of all of us. You're really taking good care of us today!"

"Well, it's not easy, son. Perhaps I was a bit hasty. Although we can provide the things we are enjoying today, we still have to purchase services. I have to pay to have grist ground at the mill. I have an account with Mr. Cutler. And another one with Doctor Prescott. But let's not talk of these things now. Better left until after this wonderful meal."

"Let me tell all of you about my bounty coat," Oliver suggested.

"What's a bounty coat?" shouted Ruthie from the other table.

"Well, the army needs coats for the soldiers, and there is no one place where they can be gotten and no money in the Continental Congress to pay for 'em even if there was somebody who could make them. So, what did they do? They are putting out a call for regular folks to make 'em. The ladies in all the local towns will be busy this winter in their kitchens spinning and weaving and sewing coats for the soldiers, and when each coat is completed it's to have a label sewn inside with the name of the town where it was made. What do you think of that?"

"Oh, I think that's a wonderful idea. Mother, can we make one."

"I don't see why not. I think that is the least we can do," responded Sarah.

"There's only one catch. . .In order for me to get one, I have to enlist for eight months. Father, I was going to tell you later, but I have already signed up."

"Oh, Oliver, I don't want to see you go again," Alethea murmured, placing her hand over his for a moment.

"Son, I don't want to see you go again either; but if you do go, I want you to be warm!"

"And," continued Oliver, "If I am killed, my heirs will be paid for the value of the coat. It's kind of like a legacy. It's also a way for the soldiers to look more alike, at least to be dressed more alike. Instead of everyone wearing their regular clothes, those with coats will look alike. Sort of like a uniform, I guess. They must have pewter buttons though."

"I think the next two or three months will be very rough on our boys in Cambridge with or without the coats," offered Benjamin as he broke another piece of bread away from the nearly finished loaf. "There probably aren't enough tents. Blankets will be in short supply, and it will be cold, bitterly cold some days. There'll be snow, of course, and our people will be wet, like as not. Food's goin' to be scarce, too. There are fewer carts taking provisions to Cambridge these days now that fall is over. I don't know how they'll survive!"

"You know, it all comes down to money, doesn't it," suggested Ebenezer. "The Continental Congress doesn't have any. Where would they get it except from the states, and the states have enough trouble supporting their own militia without sending more money to the Continental Congress to do with it what they will. I see it as a real quagmire, I do. None of us has any money."

"That is exactly why I signed up again!" exclaimed Oliver.

"I have some good news," offered Jacob. "I saw Simon in town the other day. Perhaps I shouldn't tell you. Maybe I should let Simon tell you himself, but I can't keep the secret any longer, and we need a bit of good news in this family."

"Tell us, Jacob! Out with it."

"Simon and Elizabeth are expecting a new baby! I'm sure they will tell you when they get here, so I hope you can all act surprised when they do let you know."

"Oh, I'm so happy," purred Sarah, glancing quickly to see how Mary was taking the news. Mary didn't lift her eyes from her plate, and Jacob who was sitting on the long bench beside her, gently placed his arm around her shoulders in silent support and understanding.

"Well, that is good news, indeed. Rebecca will be able to help her some, I suppose," chuckled Ebenezer, remembering what little help he and Sarah had received from their young children when a new baby arrived.

Everyone was eating more slowly now, hunger sated a bit. Sarah and Mary began clearing away some of the empty meat trays while Persis and Alethea pulled pies from the oven, cut them and placed them on the still heavily laden table in front of the men. Ruthie refilled cider mugs with warm brew and returned to her seat at the table with Ede and Jacob, Jr. The children, whispering among themselves, were looking forward to whatever the rest of the day would bring.

The meal finally at an end, the men, followed by George, left the kitchen and went into the front room. The fire there was beginning to sputter, and Ebenezer bent to add another log, poking the embers to encourage an amber burst of flame that would soon send warmth to the outside walls of the room, "If I had any tobacco, I would smoke it, and if I had any rum, I would drink it just about now. But as I have neither, I will just bring up my chair to the fire, and you boys can just do the same." Ebenezer's tobacco box sat on the mantel, a gentle reminder of earlier days when such luxuries were more readily available and affordable.

Each wall was lined with straight-backed, rush-bottomed chairs except where windows where placed, two on the front of the house and one on the side. A looking glass hung over the simple fireplace mantel on which were placed an assortment of pewter and wooden items that had come from Ebenezer's father's house. An oil lamp rested on a pine table, and a dresser rested along the interior wall. A tea kettle sat on the heath. In the background could be heard melodic voices of the women and children still working in the kitchen. Ebenezer heard the cellar door open and knew that Ruthie and the other young children had gone downstairs to gather up more apples and chestnut and hickory nuts for roasting.

"I'm sorry that Simon isn't here yet. I like to talk with all of you about important matters while you are all together, but I know he will be along shortly. Oliver, we know what your plans are, but I don't know about you Jacob, and, Benjamin, you haven't spoken of your plans of late either," began Ebenezer.

Jacob pulled a chair closer to the fire, "Father, I have given this matter a lot of thought, and I for one plan to enlist again. I am not sure when, but it will be a while. I can't leave Mary just yet. She is taking little Sarah's death something awful. She doesn't sleep, and you saw how she picked at her food today. She helped Mother take care of Samuel when he was sick, and his death upset her a lot too. I think I am needed here for a while. Doesn't look like much will be happening this winter anyway, at least from what I hear. The British are holed up; they'll spend the winter reveling and rabble-rousing in Boston, and our boys will spend the winter watching them from behind the defense line and wondering where their next meal will come from. There won't be much fighting going on."

"I'm going to sign up pretty soon. Frankly," paused Benjamin, "I need the money. There is no work around here, and I need money so that Persis and I can get married and start our own family. Perhaps if I go soon, I'll be back in time to help you with the planting, and I will be able to give you and Mother some money for your expenses too. I want to do my fair share around here. You shouldn't have to still be feeding me!"

"Benjamin, your mother and I are glad to have you and Oliver around for as long as you want to stay. Don't forget, you help me in many ways. I don't know what I would do without the help from all of you boys! Don't you think for a minute that I can do without any of you!"

"You know, we can't even be sure that we will be paid," Benjamin commented woefully, "But we have to take that chance."

"I still wish I could go with you," Ebenezer spoke quietly, thinking back on the zeal he had felt a few short months ago. The energy he had felt then was now a thing of the past. His new concern was money. He had accounts all over town that the boys knew nothing about, and he feared for the future, especially if this war were to last for any length of time. It had already lasted much longer than anyone could have imagined. He was rich, all right. Rich in land, richer than he ever thought he would be, but, he thought, you can't pay bills with land!

Silence fell upon the room as each of the four Patch men thought about his own unique circumstances. Light dancing from the flames played off their faces, accentuating the lines and crevices on each face created by weather and worry. The kitchen was quieter now. The women and girls had cleared away the residual scraps from the meal, and the children were huddled in a semicircle on the hearth before the big fireplace. Green apples hung by strings over that part of the fire that had turned to a mass of dying orange embers, and juice was beginning to ooze, sputtering in the heat as it dropped down on the graying coals below. Hickory nuts and chestnuts, also roasting, were popping their shells, scattering ashes into the mugs of amber cider warming on the hearth.

Waking from a dog nap, George stretched, yawned and wandered slowly and silently from the front room. His ears now pointing skyward, a slow, low growl began to arise from deep in this throat. "Here come Simon and Elizabeth! They're coming now!" Ruthie exclaimed, jumping to her feet and heading to the kitchen door at the east side of the house.

At that moment the door flew open, and Elizabeth, as beauteous as ever, glided into the room with Simon and the children trailing immediately behind her. She seems radiant, Jacob thought, more lovely than I even remembered! Elizabeth quickly embraced everyone with a particularly long and understanding embrace for Mary whose recent tragedy had pierced her own soul with a special sadness. I love my Mary, Jacob pondered, more than life itself. She is the mother of my children, but there will always be a special place in my heart for Elizabeth Williams. She fills a room with her presence like no other person can. She is elegant and seems possessed with a serene magic that ignites joy in others.

For a moment no one said a word, then Ede went over to Elizabeth, placing her little hands on her belly, "We know about the baby," she said.

Everyone roared with laughter. Jacob, apologizing for telling the secret, was immediately forgiven by Simon and Elizabeth. There was more hugging and kisses all around. Little Simon immediately ran to play with the other children who were more interested in the hickory nuts than all the talk about babies.

"This is a time for celebration," said Ebenezer, even his mood brightening at the sight of his ravishing daughter-in-law. "I wish someone here could play the fife, and we could have some music."

"We can have music, Papa," offered Ruthie. "Oliver, dance with me and then everyone can clap their hands!"

Oliver sprang to his feet and began to do a little jig with Ruthie following his steps as best as she could. Even at her young age she could barely keep up with his fast paced performance. When they began to tire, the men moved the big pine table to one side of the kitchen to make room for other dances. They did a reel enjoyed by the women and then old father john and hunt the squirrel with Sarah and Ebenezer watching from the sidelines.

The moon was nearly full, casting its glow into the winter darkness, when Simon and Elizabeth and Jacob and Mary bade their goodnights. Benjamin and Oliver also left to escort their young ladies home. What a wonderful day and evening it had been, a Thanksgiving to remember always.

Chapter XVI

DORCHESTER HEIGHTS

A few days later came Christmas, and the holy days that followed were filled with prayers and reverence as was the Christian custom in New England. Frequent church services were solemn as parishioners worshipped and prayed for endurance and victory.

The British were rethinking their overall strategy and the desirability of remaining in Boston. Perhaps, they thought, New York would be the better place to wage battle. They did not want to be surprised by a repeat of the Breed's Hill fight where their losses were significant. They feared that the longer they remained in Boston, the stronger the enemy would become. Life in Boston for the British during the remainder of the winter would not be pleasant, and they found themselves razing damaged houses for firewood.

After the first of the year rumors came back to Groton that General Washington was attempting to locate more ammunition for an attack on the British in Boston. The news from Boston was grim. The soldiers were mostly idle now. The ground had frozen, and the construction of defenses had ceased. Nearly the entire town had been surrounded by the American army. Cobble Hill had been fortified, and the protection of Prospect Hill secured the Charles River. Only the hill at Dorchester remained unprotected, and General Washington was determined to secure that as well. During subsequent days the Americans, using any materials they could find, began to create a barrier on that high ground in the southeast part of Boston. They gathered wagons, logs and brush to make frames that would be filled with hay in anticipation of moving them up the hill to provide enough protection in the event of a British invasion. If that were to occur, Washington planned to make a direct attack on Boston.

Food was scarce. Draft animals were also becoming scarce. When they had been worn out in service, they were slaughtered for food. The Old Rock Stock which had been developed by breeding the famous yellow Dane oxen with those from Devon were declining rapidly. The soldiers were cold. Despite the best efforts of George Washington, he was not able to procure enough coats and blankets for his men. His main preoccupations involved arms and ammunition. Word traveled that when the fortification was complete, Washington would need fresh troops for the fight that he hoped would drive the British back onto the ships for the sail out of Boston harbor and back to England. However, it was feared that they might just move on to New York.

The threat of hostilities was high, and an outbreak of fighting was considered inevitable. On February 6th an Act was passed by the Legislature to move the November term of the Court of General Sessions of the Peace and Court of Common Pleas from Charlestown to Groton. Sessions of the Court were held there in the First Parish Meeting House. On February 10th the official ballot by the House of Representatives shows that Oliver Prescott of Groton was chosen Brigadier General for Middlesex County.

After the arrival at the end of February of General Knox and his cadre of weaponry at Framingham, the pace of activity picked up. A call went out for another 2,000 men. Benjamin Patch answered that call and was among those who marched to Dorchester. History does not record his specific role in this mission, but we do know that he joined up with the boys from Westford and became a part of Captain John Minot's Company in Colonel Dikes Regiment.

The plan was to occupy Dorchester Heights in a single night after dark thereby surprising the British the following morning at first light as had been done at Breed's Hill. All through the night of March 3rd wagons carrying hay and barrels were hauled by oxen up the hill. Meanwhile Washington initiated intermittent cannon fire from the hills north and west of the city in order to distract the British from the frenetic activity of the Americans who were busily fortifying the Heights. During the night a terrible storm developed. Blustery winds blew throughout that night and into the next day and night. Knowing that the rebels would continue to fortify the hill despite inclement weather, General Howe made the decision to evacuate Boston.

During the next two weeks while gathering their goods and troops and as many Loyalists as they could take with them, the British continued to plunder and destroy the city. It was not until March 17th that weather and wind conditions permitted their sail from Boston Harbor.

Shortly thereafter an exuberant and triumphant Benjamin Patch headed for home with his company just in time for spring plowing. He was confident that the war would soon be over. During his absence his best friend, George, followed the heels of Ebenezer as he went about his daily chores. George never left Ebenezer's side. Sarah and Ruthie were knitting stockings for the troops, but the best news of all was that Mary was expecting a baby. Jacob was ecstatic and was even happier when he heard the good news from Benjamin about the victory in Boston. Before Benjamin left Dorchester Heights he heard rumors that some of Washington's troops would be headed for New York. He hoped that rumor that would prove to be false.

Chapter XVII

1776

Journal entries of Joseph Farwell, a soldier in Captain Williams Company Colonel Green's Regiment, confirm the accuracy of the rumor heard by Benjamin Patch that the Americans would be going to New York. In March Farwell's unit left Boston and marched by way of Norridge to New London by land and then by water to New York. His troops were stationed there in the King's barracks, and some members of this Regiment then marched toward Canada. In New York Colonel Prescott and his men from Massachusetts were stationed at Governor's Island until after the Battle of Long Island.

When the American forces were obliged to retreat from the city, Prescott withdrew his regiment so skillfully and successfully that he received public commendation from General Washington himself. News of these events, however, did not reach Groton quickly as mail was carried from New York to Boston by horseback over what was known as the Country Road, later known as the Post Road. What euphemistically had been called a road was really a bridle path, rocky, hilly and wide enough comfortably for only a single horse and filled with mud holes and ruts, making travel slow and extremely uncertain.

On July 4, 1776, the Declaration of Independence was signed in Philadelphia, but it was not until July 9 when news of the signing reached New York where the document was read before the American troops on the parade ground. On July 17th John Avery in Boston ordered that the Declaration of Independence be published with copies sent to the ministers of each parish of every denomination in the colony of Massachusetts.

Ministers were required to read the document to the congregations as soon as "Divine service is ended in the afternoon of the first Lord's Day after they shall have received it, and after such publication thereof to Deliver the said Declaration to the clerks of their several Towns or Districts who are hereby required to record the same. . ."

The next day, on July 18th the Declaration was read from the east balcony of the Old State House in Boston by William Greenleaf, Sheriff. All of the troops remaining in the vicinity of Boston were paraded on State Street. At the conclusion of the ceremony thirteen volleys were fired to commemorate the thirteen colonies,

* * *

Members of the Patch family had gone about their daily chores as they had in years past, clearing brush, plowing, planting and weeding. They did not learn of the Declaration of Independence until it was read in church on that memorable July Sunday morning. The service concluded, parishioners congregated on the gently sloping, grass-green expanse in front of the church.

"Well, what do you think of that?" mused Ebenezer to no one in particular as he walked down the steps of the church. On this Sunday he had not drifted off to sleep as he often did during Reverend Chaplin's monologues. Today after the sermon, he had heard the most stirring and uplifting speech he had ever listened to. It would take some time to fully comprehend it. The church had been hot and stuffy. After all it was summer just after midday. The overwhelming heat of the day would not be felt until much later in the afternoon.

He took a deep breath enjoying the sounds of nature and listening to the chatter of folks as they left the church and drifted around the adjoining grounds, huddling in groups. Some of the young men were hooting and hollering, their voices rising above the rest, "Yes! Down with the King, down with the King," they chanted. Some of the phrases Ebenezer had heard in the speech raced through his mind as he stood waiting for his family to exit the church, 'Tyranny. . .repeated injuries.

Plundered. . .ravaged. . .burnt. . .destroyed. Pledge. . .sacred honor'. Ah, yes, he thought. What he had heard mirrored what he had been thinking and feeling all these many months. The list of complaints about the actions of King George was even longer than he had imagined. 'Long train of abuses'. Yes, that is what it had been indeed. '...unfit to be the rule of a free people'. We are going to be in this for the long haul; we are indeed, he thought.

As he turned back toward the church he could see Sarah with Ruthie and Ede at her side. Sarah was standing on the steps talking with Reverend Chaplin. He could see Mary right behind her with Jacob. And, oh, yes, here come Oliver and Benjamin, too. We can talk about this on the ride home. Come on, let's go! Simon probably doesn't know about this yet. Elizabeth's baby is due any day now, and they will be staying close to home.

On Sundays or whenever the entire family went to town, Ebenezer hitched his horses up to the wagon which was large enough to accommodate everyone. On the drive home, Sarah and the girls rode in back while Ebenezer and his boys were up front, Benjamin and Ebenezer sitting on the front seat with Oliver right behind.

"Jacob said that he thinks the war is just beginning since it now involves all of the colonies, not just New England," offered Benjamin.

"I'm afraid he is probably right. Once the King and Parliament hear about what's happened, they're likely to be very angry. They'll probably send more troops and impose more hardships through more tariffs, embargoes, and heaven's only knows what else they will do. We are in it now for better or worse. As Mr. Hancock said, we 'pledge to each other our lives, our fortunes and our sacred honor'. That's a very powerful statement."

"He also referred to the 'united colonies'," offered Oliver anxious to be making a contribution to this conversation. "What does he mean by that, Father, when he also said we 'ought to be free and independent states'? I'm not sure I understand."

"Seems to me," Ebenezer replied, "that it means our colonies are all tied together in this. We're no longer states independent of each another making all of our decisions independently, at least in this matter and for this time. But as states united, we seek independence from the King. Seems to me that General Washington kind of started to do that by coming in as commander of the army and becoming the leader of all our militias from all of our colonies. On the other hand he talked about 'liberty'. We all know what that means. It will take time to sort it all out."

"Hmmm. I wonder what that will mean for the future. How will we as a people decide things for ourselves if our colonies are united and decisions made for us somehow like General Washington is making decisions for our militia," Oliver continued, feeling a bit heady by being able to put into words thoughts that might test his father's cognitive skills.

Silence prevailed as the trusty pair of horses slowly moved the wagon toward home. The clip-clop of their hooves was a comforting sound, and soon Ruthie and Ede were sound asleep in the soft, nurturing bed of sweet-smelling hay in the back of the wagon. Sarah sat with head bowed so that the brim of her bonnet shielded her face from the high-in-the-sky noonday sun, the men folks deep in their individual thoughts.

* * *

It was on July 19, 1776, when Simon and Elizabeth's new baby boy came into the world. He was named Samuel after Sarah's little Samuel, so tragically and so recently lost. Elizabeth's mother had come down to Ashby a few days earlier to be on hand to help out. Not wanting to leave Elizabeth's side for even a minute, Simon had been staying at home and was not aware of the tumultuous events that had occurred in the outside world until Benjamin rode up the next day to inquire about Elizabeth and the new baby and share news of the day.

"There's fighting in New York, Simon," offered Benjamin as he dropped the reins from his horse, allowing him to graze. "They say that some of our boys after leaving Boston marched for New York. That was back in March! They went by way of Norridge to New London by land and then by water to New York where they were stationed in what they call the Kings's Barracks. Some of them marched to Canada from there! Imagine that. Some of the others left behind joined up with Colonel Ward's Regiment."

"There's bound to be another call-up soon," concluded Simon after hearing about the Declaration document and his father's comments about new troops being needed.

"I agree. I don't think I should go just yet," offered Benjamin. "I don't think Father is well. He has no energy, and sometimes he has trouble getting his breath. I'm worried about him. He won't admit to feeling poorly, but he needs more and more help around the farm. I think he will need me for a while, but I think Oliver wants to go. Jacob seems to think this might be a good time for him to go too. Mary's baby will come soon; and if Mother can go up to help out when the time comes, he is ready. Money is pretty short for him and with the new baby. . . I don't have to tell you. You know all about it."

"Perhaps this is the time when I should go too," Simon said quietly. "I hate leaving Elizabeth now, but we need the money too. Crops were so poor last year that we are really short. Yes, tell everyone that I'll go with the next call-up. I'm sure that Stephen will go now as well." And so it was decided that Simon and Jacob would reenlist in the army as soon as possible. As Simon watched Benjamin and his horse head on down the road, he turned toward the house, dreading what he was about to tell his wife.

A few days later, on August 5, 1887, Jacob and Mary Patch became the proud parents of their new baby son, Jesse.

Benjamin visited Ashby again in mid-September after he learned about the terrible battle at Long Island. "It was real bad, I guess," he offered. "Toward the end of the month our troops sneaked out of Long Island in the night and went into the city. They stayed there about two weeks. Then the British drove them out, and they went to a place called Harlem Heights. Some of the boys were sent on a scouting party. They stayed at Harlem Heights for a few days and then went to Frogs' Point. It doesn't sound good at all. What do you suppose will happen next. I didn't tell all this to Father. I was afraid it would upset him."

Dr. Oliver Prescott, now Brigadier General, was the brother of Colonel William Prescott of what became known as Bunker Hill fame, and it fell upon the good doctor's shoulders to order out the militia. He did so on Thursday September 26th in response to orders he had received two days earlier for every fifth able-bodied man under fifty years of age who were ". . .agreeable to the Resolves of the General Assembly of this State. . ."

Nine companies were formed into a single regiment, and he appointed Eleazer Brooks and Micah Stone as colonels, Eben Bancroft as major, Mr. Moses Adams as chaplain, Mr. Joseph Hunt as surgeon mate, Daniel Loring as Adjudicant and Samuel Hartwell, quartermaster. The Seventh Company comprised men from Groton, Pepperell, Townsend and Ashby under the leadership of Captain Thomas Warren. Eight of the men were from Ashby, seventeen from Pepperell, fifteen from Townsend and the rest from Groton, making a total of sixty nine in Company Seven including Jacob and Simon Patch. There were 627 men drafted from the area that day.

Doctor Prescott directed Colonel Brooks to order the various captains to march their companies as soon as possible on the "best and most proper road to Horse Neck". They were ordered to march the following Saturday. Captain Warren ordered his men to meet on the green in Groton at sunup on Saturday prepared to march. He told them that it would probably take about eleven days to reach their destination. They would not reach New York until mid October.

CHAPTER XVIII

NATHAN HALE

During the early part of September General Washington's army was spread out from the Battery to Kings Bridge with the British in ships bordering them on the southern part of Long Island to a point opposite Harlem Heights. The Americans were incredibly vulnerable, not knowing what General Howe's next move would be.

Again Washington needed a spy, someone who could infiltrate enemy lines and collect information that would be of value to him, such as the strength of the enemy in numbers and its plans. He needed a capable individual and asked for volunteers. Not one stepped up until a young, tall captain named Nathan Hale came forward. His comrades attempted to discourage him; but in his low, musical voice he said, "I think I owe to my country the accomplishment of an object so important, and so much desired by the Commander of her armies. . . I wish to be useful, and every kind of service necessary for the public good becomes honorable by being necessary."

Although he had been feeble as a child, Nathan Hale had grown into a perfectly proportioned individual with a broad chest and firm muscles. Just twenty one years of age, this blue-eyed Connecticut soldier had been prepared for college by his village minister, and he graduated from Yale in the class of 1773. Known for his charming, benign manner, he taught school for six months in a little red school house on the banks of the Connecticut River. In 1775 he was commissioned as a first lieutenant and was promoted to captain after participating in the siege of Boston. General Washington accepted this young volunteer and ordered the American vessels in Long Island Sound to carry him from the camp at Harlem Heights across to Long Island.

Disguised as a school teacher, Hale was able to enter the British lines on September 12th while British ships cruised up and down the East River. For nearly ten days he virtually dropped out of sight, gathering information as he safely moved about through the British camp. He made drawings of enemy fortifications with descriptions and notes on enemy strength written in Latin. Then he crossed the East River and traveled through the woods until he reached a point of safety on the shore near Huntington where he had first landed.

It had been previously arranged that a boat would meet him there and take him back over to Connecticut. Unfortunately, he was captured there on Saturday, September 21st. Had he not run from his captors when ordered to halt, he might have avoided capture. The documents so carefully obtained were found under the inner soles of his shoes. In the lining of his coat was found his Yale diploma.

That same day he was taken to New York where 493 houses were on fire, and where nearly one-third of the city was in ashes. When he was turned over to General Howe, he immediately identified himself, admitting the purpose of his mission and to being a spy. He bemoaned that his hope of serving his country had been thwarted. Howe suggested that he would consider a full pardon if Hale would accept the rank of captain in the British army.

Hale did not reply. Because there was no response, Howe correctly assumed that Hale was unwilling to accept his offer and ordered that his execution take place the next day without benefit of military trial. William Cunningham, the infamous Provost Marshal of the Royal Army, was directed to receive into custody Nathan Hale, a captain in the rebel army, convicted that day of being a spy. It was further ordered that Hale be hung by the neck until dead the following morning at day break.

The next day, Sunday, September 22nd, was sunny. Hale's requests for a clergyman and a bible were refused. After spending the night in the Sugar House Prison in New York, at eleven o'clock in the morning he was taken to the hanging noose. As he stepped forward, he handed the provost marshal several letters he had written during the night to his mother, two sisters and a friend.

Looking out across the vast sea of onlooking Redcoats as the noose was placed around his neck, he spoke those fourteen words that history would forever record, "I only regret that I have but one life to lose for my country." His body was never found. The letters he had written were torn up by the provost marshal and scattered by the winds, and the intelligence he so meticulously gathered never reached General Washington.

Chapter XIX

THE MARCH

The march to Horse Neck by Captain Warren and his company was relatively uneventful. The troops camped in fields at night. Oxen pulled carts containing food and other supplies over barely passable roads. Captain Warren rode by horseback. During evenings when they camped near a tavern, those men who carried a few pence frequented that local establishment to enjoy music and merriment.

Fortunately the weather was ideal for marching with warm days and cool nights. The fall rains had not yet begun. Jacob and Simon were familiar with the route to Sudbury as they had traveled that route on their march to Lexington, and they had been to Boston on several occasions.

At Sudbury the company turned southwest onto the relatively well-traveled Country Road, the road that post riders used in carrying mail from New York and Philadelphia to Boston and that would take the militia very close to Horse Neck. This was terrain Jacob and Simon had never seen before. It appeared to have been laid out without bounds or compass following Indian trails. Sudbury's location was at a crossroads of trails and roads that made it the most populous town in Middlesex County. The troops were amazed by the level of human activity in this town so far from Boston.

From Sudbury they traveled westward through Marlborough, Northborough and Shrewsbury where Farrar's Tavern was another place of great activity. Behind the main building housing the tavern itself was a large shed for wagons and another serving as shelter for teamsters who were traveling through.

The Post Road went through the center of each town through which it passed, enabling travelers to view the daily activities of the folks living in houses bordering tree-lined streets. These streets became a bit wider within the towns themselves. Each town had one or more meeting houses, a common or green and an adjoining burying ground, usually an inn, a tavern and sometimes a shop or two. Although variable in size, house lots were large enough for a house, outbuildings and a garden at the very least.

People came out onto the streets as troops marched through, cheering them on. Worchester, another crossroads of trails and roads, had several taverns; one of them, the Jones' Tavern was a haven for Tories, but the tavern owned by Luke Brown became headquarters for the patriots and provided a respite for Company Seven, offering dried meat and cider for everyone.

Leaving Worcester the Post Road traversed through Cherry Valley and passed by the turnoff to the Old Post Road that would have been a shorter route but much more difficult for marching and virtually impassible for horses and oxen. In Brookfield the company was again cheered on by a huge crowd, rallying in the common. In Warren the Post Road paralleled the Inaboag River for about two miles along the northern edge of the town, bypassing the center of town and the meeting house, unlike the route experienced so far that merely passed through the centers of towns. Going south of the town part of the road was very passable, but in other areas mounting the hills was extremely difficult, particularly for the supply-ladden carts. While in the plain they passed a lovely fresh water pond where water supplies were replenished for both man and beast.

Passing through the outer commons and that third band of terrain from the Connecticut River, characterized by hilly, rocky and steep land, they continued for several miles. The trees were a mixture of pine and oak, the countryside, stony, barren and uninhabited. It was worthless land, thought Simon Patch, although the views from the hilltops were spectacular. After this eight mile stretch, they crossed the Chicopee River in Palmer and headed toward what was known as the Springfield Plain, where the road passed along the banks of the Chicopee and then uphill toward Springfield where only a couple of months earlier an arsenal and armory had been established at the top of the hill.

The direction of the route changed at Springfield going more directly south through West Springfield. The west side of the road was bounded by the southern end of the Holyoke range of hills, and they crossed the newly constructed bridge over the river there. As they traveled out of Massachusetts into Connecticut, they began to see elevated river banks not seen before, and neither plains nor meadows were evident. In Suffield there was a long, broad green through the center of the town, and for the first time they saw extensive tobacco fields. How different this terrain was in appearance from the land they knew and loved back home!

Heading toward Hartford they passed through the picturesque town of Windsor which lay on both sides of the river. The road from Windsor to Hartford passed through the Connecticut Valley with its backdrop of graceful hills and gently rolling countryside, still green and lush even though late summer was slowly drifting into fall. The troops from time to time passed cart loads of grain, pork, beef and cattle, the main products of trade between Boston and Hartford.

In Hartford they saw other troop companies, also on their trek to New York, as this town was the main route between the east and the Hudson River valley area. The main street here was in extremely poor condition from high intensity traffic, even though a more passable road had been constructed earlier over a swamp to accommodate horses and oxen.

The next town they came to was Wethersfield, one of the oldest settlements in Connecticut. The road passed the Hartford Road and from there took several turns before leaving town. The town was surrounded by lush meadow lands. Its center boasted the widest expanse of a green the troops had seen thus far, and the meeting house featured a classically elegant Christopher Wren spire. Jacob was reminded of the one on the South Church in Boston that had been constructed about fifteen years earlier. Wethersfield had more than one ferry as the town lay on both sides of the river, and there were several taverns. Everyone in the company marveled at the fertile land which lay in this river valley all the way to Middletown, and the daytime weather was notably warmer, so unlike Massachusetts at this time of year.

The road passing through this stretch was the best the company had encountered. It was relatively smooth; they were no longer stumbling over rocks and stones. The foliage was more lush. The trees were huge, soaring to a height of 100 to 150 feet and two to five feet in diameter. Off to the side fallen trees were in all stages of decomposition, many now covered with vines. Bushes hugged the road, encroaching onto the pathway. Along the way could be seen old Indian trails crisscrossing through the underbrush, avoiding as much as possible the swamps and marshes arising from what would be the high water table in spring time and to more easily cross the streams that meandered through the area.

Up until now the roads had been just wide swaths cut through the forest with half-buried boulders and tree stumps sticking up here and there. Small streams often ran through or across the road bed. During the summer growing season new shoots had sprang up, now grown enough to trip up the feet of horses and men. High winds often brought down large trees that fell across the pathway, impeding the travel of the troops and their supply carts.

After passing through Middletown, the company very soon came to Durham. It seemed to both Simon and Jacob that this town was nearly the size of Groton. Here flax seemed to be one of the principal crops. It obviously was an important stopping off place and, they were told, lay about half way between Hartford and New Haven. The troops were also told that six four-horse stages usually passed through town daily and stopped at the Swathel Inn. A company of Connecticut militia passed through town, coming from the east while Company Seven was traveling from the north. It was another crossroads town.

The march from Durham to New Haven took nearly a full day but was a much more pleasant experience. Clearly, we are traveling closer to the coast, they thought. Highways seemed less important to these folks as they could travel and trade along the water. However, these roads were much wider, though less clearly defined, than what they had experienced further inland. They had likely been laid out when land was less costly.

As the company approached North Haven, they traveled through the valley of the Quinnipiac River with its great meadows covering deposits of clay. There were mills lining the shores of the Muddy River where workers seemed to be building small, seagoing craft. The men breathed deeply to enjoy the damp salt air. East Rock towered overhead.

A little further along they were able to cross the Mill River on a cart bridge and continue along the marsh to the west of New Haven and up over the summit of Milford Hill. After crossing the river on the West Bridge, they traveled about one and a half miles to the New Haven town green.

What an amazing green, they thought. "We don't have fields this large at home," said Simon aloud to himself in incredulous disbelief. Clearly this area had been the center of town for many, many years. It was large enough for the whole town to assemble to share the news of the day and to rally for other events!

For the rest of the trip it was apparent that they would be traveling along the coast. The weather was balmy with heavy fog in the early hours of each day. They forded the many rivers that flowed into Long Island Sound. As they approached Milford they crossed the Housatonic River over the Meeting-House Bridge, following the road down to the First Congregational Church. The towns were closer together now. In Stratford they passed the seventy milestone.

Below Fairfield on the way to Norwalk, they encountered another stretch of bad road. Leaving the town on the hill, they wended their way down a steep slope and crossed over a bridge. The landscape, they thought, was truly astounding, nothing like what they had left behind back at home.

It was not until they reached Norwalk that they first heard of a young soldier named Nathan Hale. They were told that during the middle of September Hale had come to Norwalk to obtain a vessel to carry him across the Sound. He said good-bye to his companion, Sergeant John Hempstead of his own company of Knowlton's Rangers, and was taken across to Huntington, Long Island, by a Captain Pond in the sloop "Schuyler". He was never seen again.

Stamford and Darien were known as havens for Tories and Loyalists. The company passed through these towns during the night as unobtrusively as possible so as not to create trouble or arouse suspicion. Even by moonlight the majesty of the great trees lining the street in Stamford was evident. Captain Warren's Company arrived at Horse Neck mid-afternoon the next day. They had marched about twenty miles a day for the entire trip. In the flat lands they were able to march a little further each day, but they had lost time traveling through Massachusetts where the road and terrain were much more difficult.

Both Jacob and Simon were exhausted from the extended period of sustained travel. They were nursing painfully blistered feet. Some in the company had worn their shoes completely through. Some days had been rainy, and they had marched in cold wet clothing. But those days had been very few. Early fall, they readily agreed, is just about the most divine time of year. Both Jacob and Simon had been struck by the cascading colors of the fall foliage that appeared to change right before their eyes as they traveled. Fallen leaves had crunched comfortingly beneath their feet.

While marching all day, they were able to notice the transformation of their natural surroundings whereas, when at home, demands of the day required their focus, and they couldn't take time to appreciate the grandeur around them. Adjacent to the marshes, red maples were ablaze with their brightest magenta. The ashes were turning characteristic process yellow. Some of the birches had already dropped their leaves. Oak leaves had not yet turned russet and would hold their leaves until after the first snow fall. The array of colors had been punctuated by mile after mile of pine and other bluish-viridian evergreens. All in all, they felt very fortunate. At Horse Neck they would meet up with other companies in Colonel Brooks Regiment before the march to New York.

CHAPTER XX

NEW YORK

General George Washington had retreated from Long Island on August 27th. Although his desire was to completely evacuate Manhattan Island, the Council of General Officers, with whom he was required to consult, recommended that he hold his position. Congress had resolved on October 11 that ". . .by every art and by whatever expense, to obstruct effectually the navigation of the river between Fort Washington and Mount Constitution (Fort Lee)."

However, after the landing of a large British force on Frogs' Neck, it had become necessary to retreat quickly after three men-of-war had passed through the obstructions. The British by then were at Tarrytown and were ready to unload men and arms. They would be rallying the Loyalists to rise up against the rebels.

The days that followed were filled with anxiety. Washington's despair was reflected in his general orders, ". . .How much better will it be to die honorably fighting in the field, than to return home covered with shame and disgrace, even if the cruelty of the enemy should allow you to return. A brave and gallant behavior for a few days and patience under some little hardships, may save our country and enable us to go into winter quarters with safety and honor."

His troops were discouraged, knowing that their fate was uncertain. The various regiments had been hastily thrown together during a period of temporary enthusiasm. Now the troops began to experience the true sacrifices and hardships of a soldier's life. Many were sick, but there were few medical facilities. Dysentery and typhoid abounded. The troops had been defeated and forced to flee from Long Island although they had achieved a modest victory at Harlem Heights.

They remained in disarray. When they came together, the senior officers among them took charge of any men in the vicinity, creating disruptive jealousies that threatened to tear the army apart. It would not be until the middle of October when Washington would be able to separate his army into divisions under major generals and brigades under brigadier generals with their commands clearly defined.

However, the army continued to remain undisciplined, poorly armed and lacking in adequate transportation. The enemy on the other hand was well armed, well trained and had access to an immense fleet of vessels, giving it superiority on the waters. Generally such an imbalance of relative strengths could have given General Howe and the British easy victories over George Washington's inadequate army on many occasions, any one of which would have ended the war right then and there.

Washington's disadvantage on Long Island was so significant that his only means of retreat was north to King's Bridge which was protected by Fort Independence. Howe decided to divide his forces, leaving half of them in New York and transporting the other half up the rivers. Any attempt to land on shore would be detected by the Americans who patrolled the Harlem and East Rivers and obstructed the roads leading to their camps. On September 22nd a small band of British had attempted to land at Randall's Island, resulting in a deadly skirmish.

The most advantageous point for landing a large group of the enemy was at Frogs' Neck, projecting about two miles into Long Island Sound and from which a bridge led directly to King's Bridge. At the village of Westchester the road ran over a causeway that had been the dam for a mill on the west side of town. It had two openings, one for the overflow and another that formed an outlet from the mill pond. Both openings were covered by planks, forming a bridge over which one had to pass to reach King's Bridge.

The Americans recognized the importance of this bridge. On the west side of the causeway was a large pile of cordwood that created a natural protective barrier for the twenty Continental Army riflemen posted there. They were ordered to defend the causeway and to remove the planks over the openings if the British approached. Somewhat further east was another point where the water could be forded, and another group of soldiers was placed at that point to prevent the British from reaching the road that led to Eastchester.

The morning of Saturday, October 12th was warm. Heavy fog lay over the water concealing it from the road. When the fog lifted, a double line of barges and a man-of-war loaded with Redcoats, horses and artillery came into view. The British landed 4,000 men in a cove where the road ran to the edge of the water. They wasted no time in forming into regiments and in marching over Frogs' Neck Road toward the causeway.

Moving rapidly, they appeared to be familiar with the landscape. By the time they reached the causeway, the planks had been removed, and the small band of American soldiers hiding behind the woodpile began firing with all their might. The British became so confused that they retreated to higher ground. The group of British who attempted to cross at the ford were also driven back by the Americans.

That an American force of two dozen soldiers was able to hold at bay a British army of 4,000 men for several hours speaks well of the bravery and strategy of Washington's relatively defenseless band of troops. The General's victories were gained by wits and common sense and certainly not by strength of force.

Once on higher ground the British were able to put up a fierce struggle, and both sides were reinforced with additional troops as the day wore on. By the end of the day a large part of the American army confronted General Howe at this point. The best defense for the Americans was the ability of these troops to utilize such defenses as stone walls and trees for protection as skirmishes continued. It is highly likely that the Massachusetts companies had now joined up with the Washington army.

General Heath had command of the American troops in Westchester County until the arrival of General Charles Lee on Monday, October 14th, but General Heath was asked to retain command until General Lee could familiarize himself with his surroundings. A Massachusetts farmer, General William Heath had been active in military affairs for many years and had as recently as August been promoted to Major General. Yet General Washington had doubts about his abilities.

British born General Lee had come to America to serve in the French and Indian War after which he moved to Virginia and, through his experiences there, ultimately became a supporter of colonial independence. Over the years he had gained considerable military experience. Lee was ambitious and hoped to displace George Washington as commander-in-chief.

The command consisted of three brigades under Brigadier Generals Nixon, McDougall and James Clinton whose command was temporarily under the direction of Colonel John Glover. Lee's headquarters were at Valentine's Hill with the Nixon brigade. As the landing of the British at Pell's Point had been anticipated, Colonel Glover was sent to guard the roads leading from that point to the rear of the American forces. He camped near the Boston Post Road slightly north of Eastchester.

On the morning of October 16th Washington and his generals scouted out Pell's Point as deserters from the British army had told him that General Howe was planning to move his troops there. Upon returning to camp, Washington determined that "Fort Washington must be retained as long as possible." The next day orders were issued for the retreat from King's Bridge. The retreat was slow and laborious through the hills west of the Bronx. Troops were spread out across the countryside. The terrain was inhospitable with narrow farm roads between high hills.

Wagons and horses were in short supply, necessitating transportation of arms and artillery by relay system. After a day's trip the wagons would leave their cargo with guards, and it would remain there until the next relay could move it forward. Progress was so slow that Washington did not reach Valentine's Hill until three days after Howe had landed.

Had the British chosen to attack at that point, the result would have been disastrous for the 1,100 Americans then fit for duty, constituting only one of the four regiments under Colonel Glover's command. Glover's camp fortunately was located within view of the Boston Post Road and the bridge over the Hutchinson River. It was also within cannon shot of Wolf's Lane, the only road from Pell's Point. Because of the salt marsh and the river, the road was the only means of approach for the enemy. The road behind him, the road from Eastchester to White Plains, was Glover's only means of retreat to the main army which was moving north a few miles to the west.

After six days General Howe realized that there were no American troops stationed at Pell's Point, about three miles north. On October 18th light infantry, grenadiers and some German Jagers embarked on the south side of Frogs' Neck on flat boats and moved around the point into Eastchester Bay. Meanwhile Howe's main army ferried across Hutchinson's River, landing near the Shore Road. After another serious setback, Howe was able to cross rapidly to the Bronx and beyond to Eastchester where he was able to prevent passage of the Americans. He then moved slowly to White Plains.

On the night of October 18th Colonel Glover retreated from the Bronx, leaving the east part of the country open to the British. Had the British passed over the bridge north of the American position, the line of retreat would have been cut off. Alternatively General Howe kept his army in camp along the Boston Post Road where it was reinforced during the next couple of days. While Howe was slowly gathering his forces, Washington's army was laboriously moving northward over a landscape not understood by those in command as they were without maps.

A Committee of the New York Provincial Congress suggested that Washington take his supplies and equipment to White Plains, and he subsequently sent Colonel Rufus Putnam on a scouting mission during the night of October 19th to determine the lay of the land. Putnam, another veteran of the French and Indian War, was also from Massachusetts. He reported that the British had landed on Pell's Point. Skirmishes occurred during the afternoon between part of Glover's brigade and some of the enemy's advance parties near Eastchester.

The next morning Putnam with Colonel Reed, the adjutant general, and a group of twenty soldiers went by horseback to survey Eastchester. Separating himself from Colonel Reed and the soldiers, Putnam disguised himself and started out on the road to White Plains. At a fork in the road, he headed to the right, leading to a house where a woman told him that he was headed for New Rochelle and that the British were there.

He retraced his steps taking the other turn at the fork in the road that went to White Plains. He passed many deserted houses until he came upon one surrounded by men whom he determined were not British. Approaching with caution and asking questions, he learned that most of the British were at New Rochelle, about nine miles from White Plains over a good, flat road. He also learned that there was a substantial quantity of arms at White Plains with only a small militia to defend them.

Additionally the British had another detachment only about five miles from White Plains toward the North River where they also had ships and tenders. With this information, Putnam headed back to headquarters by way of the Bronx where Americans were situated on the western heights. By then it was after sunset. Traveling at night through Tory country, he apparently was guided by good fortune to the headquarters near King's Bridge and reported to the General, giving him a sketch of the country.

A few hours later Putnam was ordered to return to the Bronx, and he arrived there about two o'clock in the morning. On the morning of October 21st the Bronx division marched before daylight for White Plains, arriving about nine o'clock in the morning. The same morning General Washington rode to White Plains where the division from the Bronx had arrived before him. The stores that had been housed there for safekeeping were guarded by Graham's militia, a regiment of fewer than 300 men.

Later in the day at about four o'clock in the afternoon the last American division under General Heath left the vicinity of King's Bridge, leaving 600 men in charge of the barracks and the stores remaining at the evacuated camp. Heath marched all night, passing Valentine's Hill at eight in the evening and reaching Chatterton Hill at four the following morning. On October 23rd Washington established his headquarters at White Plains on the plains near the cross roads and remained there until October 28th when the enemy approached. The camp was then relocated to North Castle.

Meanwhile a regiment of Loyalists was recruited from the general area and placed under the enemy command of Colonel Robert Rogers. When the Americans learned of this, 750 men were ordered to initiate a surprise attack during the following night. Unfortunately, the attack occurred during a change of sentries, and the surprise was not entirely successful. However, many of the men in the Roger's regiment were roughed up, and several were killed or wounded.

The American troops then returned with arms and thirty one prisoners, all of whom turned out to be Americans! During this same period of time General Howe continued to amass his troops that remained scattered throughout the surrounding towns. Another 8,000 men arrived by flatboats from New York.

His order dated October 27th commanded that his troops to be ready to march at six in the morning in two columns, and with this order movement of the British troops toward White Plains began. Both columns took the same road until it branched, and the two columns then took separate roads with the second column taking the Old York Road.

An American column under General Lee was comprised of six New England regiments, and about 1,500 men under General Spencer had been sent down to intercept the British. They occupied high ground about midway between the two roads on which the British were marching northward. The enemy was met a little after nine in the morning.

Spencer's troops, using stone walls for protection, fired heavily. The enemy troops hesitated. The Hessians scattered into the fields, threatening the Americans who also scattered, many not returning to camp until much later in the day. Twelve Americans were killed; twenty three were wounded, and two became missing in this skirmish. After this episode the second British column continued its advance and later joined the first column on the plains in front of the American position.

These plains were bounded on three sides by high hills. On the west was the Bronx, behind which was Chatterton Hill and to the northwest were Purdy, Hatfield and Merritt Hills. The main road ran between Purdy and Hatfield Hills, and the Bronx River lay east of Chatterton Hill. General Washington had situated the main divisions of his army on the southern slopes of these three central hills. General Putnam's troops were on the right on Purdy Hill; General Heath's, on Hatfield Hill; and Washington's were in the middle on a gentle slope running through the village with its county court house, two churches, taverns, a few stores and houses. Merritt Hill was on the extreme left and was steep with dense underbrush, making it difficult to attack.

West of General Putnam's command was Chatterton Hill, rising to a height of 180 feet. Its lower slopes were wooded, but its upper slopes were open fields with full view of the American forces. General Heath arrived there at four o'clock in the morning on October 22nd to begin construction of an earthworks barricade on the crest of that hill. Leaving a few troops there, he continued to build entrenchments for the main part of the army on the other hills.

At the last minute, and almost as an afterthought, George Washington on October 28th sent 1,600 troops, mostly militia, including men from Maryland and Delaware under the command of General McDougall, to Chatterton Hill to join those already there. Born in Scotland General McDougall had emigrated to America as a child and had worked early in his life delivering milk in New York

City. At the age of fourteen he went to sea, remaining at sea until the death of his first wife after which he became a merchant. After the war he became a representative in the New York Continental Congress and ultimately organized and became the first president of the Bank of New York.

Chapter XXI

OCTOBER 28, 1776

It was Monday. It promised to be one of those days known in Massachusetts as Indian summer. The men in Company Seven had been marching all night. General Lee had ordered his division of 8,000 men, baggage, artillery and 150 wagons to march to North Castle to take the ground to the east and north.

After marching about three miles they could see a huge column of enemy attempting to cut them off. The American caravan turned off and marched by Dobb's Ferry road, arriving in White Plains early in the morning. General McDougall ordered his brigade of 1,600 men up Chatterton's Hill where they began to construct a defense.

* * *

Already Simon and Jacob could feel the warmth of the rising autumn sun. They lifted their faces. It felt good. It had been a long night. They had not slept, and they had not eaten. They were tired and hungry. "Do you think there'll be fighting today?" asked Jacob.

"I think there's a good chance," responded Simon wearily. "That column we saw back there must be getting closer by now. Three hills seem to be pretty well fortified. Looks like we're in a position to back up the army from where we are here when the Redcoats charge up those hills. Then I suppose we'll go on to North Castle, too."

"I hope you're right!" Simon and Jacob drifted apart, mingling with the other men in their company. Time seemed to stand still. Tensions were high. Very high. Nervous men were frantically pacing back and forth. Some were hastily gathering brush from the downhill woodland, piling it as fast as humanly possible to produce a visual barrier. Others were crouched behind the stone walls that bordered the fields, their muskets aimed down hill. They were waiting, waiting, waiting. Terror! Panic! Hearts pounding! Racing!

All of a sudden someone yelled, "Look! Look down there!" All men within hearing distance turned toward the shout. In the distance came marching in formation two columns of Redcoats and Hessians. Closer and closer they came with each passing minute. They waded through the Bronx River weapons held high. All of a sudden the enemy's columns parted. One column was coming directly toward them. Climbing the rocky slope. My God, they've seen us! What will they do next? What shall we do now?

At the hold-your-fire command, each man in the company grabbed his musket and ran for cover. But there was little of it. There had been too little time and too little man power to build adequate defenses to stave off the oncoming wall of Redcoats.

All of a sudden, a smattering of fire began. A shot here. A shot there. Now more frequent. Soon there was panic. Some men fled. Others held their positions. The air filled with dense, gray smoke. The ground trembled, and the adjacent hills steamed as though on fire. The furious sounds of battle gradually rose to a crescendo. Cannon fire roared on both sides. Fortunately many balls missed their marks and could be seen bouncing along the ground like red hot balls of flame, finally exploding into intermittent sputtering fires. The enemy cannon were located too low and could not be elevated high enough to be effective. The American cannon could not be lowered far enough.

Still the enemy ground forces kept coming up the hill. Closer and closer they came. Some were on foot; others, on horseback. So many of them. Overwhelming. No time to think. No place to hide. Cannot judge the passage of time. Seems an eternity.

Cannon balls streamed through the air, sending stones flying. Fences and stone walls were knocked down, torn to bits. Bodies were everywhere. Redcoats, Hessians and Americans. The cries of horses and the screams of men were deafening. Would it ever end.

Sounds of fire power were now echoing from the other hills coming to the aid of the small militia band on the outpost of Chatterton Hill. Smoke was becoming more dense, the odor, pungent. It filled the eyes; it filled the lungs. Too thick to see. An endless barrage of penetrating sound and a thick shower of air bourne missles. It was deafening. Are minutes passing, or are they hours?

All of a sudden out of nowhere came a crushing pain that struck Simon in the leg just below the hip. The pain only lasted a second before he was overcome with blackness. In that brief moment a colorful image flashed through his mental vision. It was his memory of Elizabeth as she stood on the rock-step of his house, waving to him on the morning he had left home to join the march. Tears had been streaming down her lovely face as she held the new baby, Samuel, in her arms. Then unconsciousness overwhelmed him.

Something whistled past Jacob's head. Too close. Much too close, he thought. He shifted his position slightly to relieve a leg cramp, waiting for another scarlet red torso to come up the hill out of the wall of smoke and into his range of fire. Time again stood still. He continued to huddle behind a large granite boulder that he believed to be his only defense.

Out of the corner of his eye he could see hand-to-hand combat between Redcoats and Americans. Flickering sunshine glistened on the arms of those brilliant red uniforms. There are so many of them and so few of us, Jacob thought. He could see gleaming bayonets slashing out at anything and everything, always seeking to penetrate tender flesh. How much longer could this go on without all of us being killed, he wondered.

When he thought he could endure no more, the sounds of cannon finally began to subside becoming more sporadic with each round. Occasional nervous musket fire could still be heard all around him. As cannon fire abated, the agonized screams of tortured men and fallen horses took center stage.

Smoke from cannon fire slowly began to dissipate into the brilliant, crystal clear blue sky. Jacob could now see around him bodies, lying silent in death or near-death. And he could hear the wailing moans of the dying and grievously wounded and the neighing of horses suffering unmercifully with the pain of broken legs and fatal wounds. These horrific sights and sounds he knew would haunt him for the rest of his life.

Jacob looked around for his comrades. There were few men in sight. He recognized no one. We're retreating, he thought. Carefully he stood up, wincing from the pain of his cramped position. Looking down hill, he could see the town burning below. The court house was in flames. Many of the other buildings were also ablaze. As he turned away in disbelief, a stranger motioned to him to follow the others who were moving back toward the Dobbs Ferry Road and over the bridge that crossed the Bronx River to relative safety in the hills about two miles from the field of battle.

By the time Jacob reached the American lines, conditions were chaotic. Everyone was shouting and pointing. There were some boys from Delaware and, oh, yes, there were some of our boys. He couldn't understand any of the conversation. People were hurling supplies from a wagon, stacking them on the ground. What are they doing, he thought. As he moved closer, he overheard conversation about someone going back for more wounded. Oh, he thought, they are going to search for any of our boys who are alive and bring them back. While they are doing that, I'll try to find my company and see if Simon is back yet.

Exhausted, he roamed around, half dazed from lack of food, water and sleep, unable to think clearly. It was late afternoon. Sunlight was beginning to fade. It looked as though they would be camping here for the night. This seemed to be farm land. Where can he be? Where is Simon? After a mug of warm cider and some very welcome bread and cheese, Jacob drifted off to sleep while sitting beneath a tree.

When he woke, it was dark, and it was raining. Someone had covered him with a blanket during the night. The camp was still bustling with activity. Doctors in their distinctive garb were roaming through the camp providing blankets and dressings to those in need. Surgeon's mates were bringing in on carts the bodies of those who had been wounded or who were too sick to walk any further. Behind the carts were tied the reins of ambulatory horses that had survived to be picked up in the field. Weapons had been confiscated, and prisoners, captured. They would go back later for the dead.

Earlier, far enough from the anticipated battle at White Plains, the Continental Army had identified a church at North Castle as an appropriate place for a hospital. Doctor James Tilton, who on January 16, 1776, had been appointed as regimental surgeon, had begun to prepare the site. Born on a farm in Dover, Delaware, Doctor Tilton had studied medicine with Doctor Ridgely, a prominent physician in Dover before graduating from the College of Philadelphia with an M.D. in 1771. After the war he returned to Dover to practice medicine.

Unfortunately, the fighting occurred before Doctor Tilton's preparations were complete. Many of the surgeons were absent, having gone off with the sick, and had not as yet returned. When Tilton learned of the fighting, he went off into the field himself along with every other available surgeon. Several mates followed with a wagon bringing instruments and dressings. They located near the lines and would remain there for about a week caring for the sick and injured.

Fewer than 100 militia were reported killed or wounded. Doctor Tilton directed medical care in the field as well as at the hospital in North Castle during that week. He was incredibly short of staff. Many of the sick and wounded who were well enough to travel would be sent to medical facilities in Stamford and Norwich, Connecticut, where they could receive more than emergency care.

* * *

"Son. Son. Can you hear me?" were the first words Simon heard as he drifted in and out of consciousness. He opened his eyes looking up into the dark, penetrating eyes of a man donned in a black hat, scarlet coat, waist coat and white shirt.

"Yes," his voice sounded so far away. It didn't sound like his voice at all. What happened to me, he thought. My leg. What is wrong with my leg? Burning with pain!

"Son, you've been hurt. You've been hit in the leg. It's pretty bad, but I am a doctor, and I am going to try to help you. You have been brought by wagon from the field. You are now in the army camp. You will be safe here. I'm going to ask the mate to bring you over to our supply tent, and I am going to try to remove what I can of the bullet."

"Where's my brother. One of my brothers is in my company," Simon tried to lift his head but fell back exhausted.

"Is he, now. We're going to have to try to find him for you. It would be nice if he could be here with you while we operate." Doctor Tilton turned away, "Cover him with a blanket, will you. He's getting wet. Then go see if you can find this lad's brother, will you?" Turning back to Simon, "What's your brother's name?"

"His name is Jacob"

"Jacob, what?"

"His name is Jacob Patch."

"Go get Jacob Patch. Don't come back without him!"

Meanwhile Jacob had located a few men from Company Seven, and together they went to the food wagon where they devoured bread and salted fish, washing it down with a pint of spruce beer each. It never tasted so good. Despite the food and drink, they were still shivering from the dampness, the rain and the cold, as they all gratefully huddled together under a make shift tent. They talked in hushed tones of the overwhelming experience they had just endured. We were so outnumbered, four to one at least. We didn't even stand a chance. Do you think the main army was attacked? What will happen next? How long is your enlistment? Is anyone missing? Mostly they, as one, speechlessly shared their all-consuming emotions.

"My brother is missing," Jacob offered, "Has anyone seen him? Simon Patch."

"No," said one of the Townsend boys, "But have you seen Tim Warren or Hinch Warren? They're missing too. Several of the Groton boys haven't turned up yet, I hear. They are in Captain Warren's Company, like me."

Off in the distance they could hear yelling. What's going on? Can you hear?

Sounds like, "Ahab, Ahab". Closer it came, and closer still. Someone is calling. "Jahab, Jahab. Hatch. Jacob Patch!" My God, that's me. What do they want, thought Jacob. He stood up, "Hey, over here. I'm Jacob Patch. What is it?"

"It's your brother. The doctor wants you to come right away." Jacob immediately recognized Mr. Joseph Hunt, surgeon's mate, from his own company!

"Oh, sweet blushing geraniums! He can't be dead!"

"No, he's alive but he's been hurt real bad. Doctor Turner's got to operate."

Jacob began to run. He could feel his heart thumping and felt hot and flushed all of a sudden with blood rushing to his head. He felt as if his heart could just jump right out of his chest. It was beating so hard. He was scared beyond words. His hands were cold. He was sweating. He was still running. Faster now. Don't let him die. Oh, please don't let him die. We can't take another loss. It would kill Mother and Father. And Elizabeth.

Up ahead he could see the medical tent. There were litters everywhere. He could hear the moans, the cries and an occasional wailing scream. Was he hearing Simon's voice above all the rest, or was it his imagination? Pausing briefly, he looked around not knowing which way to turn. The young mate who had come for him, pointed, "He's over there."

Breathlessly and in almost a single leap, Jacob was at his side. "I'm here, Simon. It's going to be all right. Yes, it is for sure." His reassuring words came automatically belying his own retched anxiety as he looked down at his helpless younger brother.

"Just stay with him," said the mate, "The doctor will be 'round as soon as he can."

Turning to Simon, "What happened?" asked Jacob.

"I have no idea. All I know is that I felt an awful pain in my leg. Everything went black. I think I woke up a little once, and I was laying in the field. There were bodies all around me, screaming and moaning. It was terrible. I can still hear it and see it. . . But I never really woke up until just a little while ago, and I was here. I have no idea how I got here. Doctor says that I'm hurt real bad. Got hit by some kind of field artillery, I guess. They are going to try to get it out, I hope."

Jacob stood beside the litter trying not to let the tears, welling up behind his eyes, spill over. He felt faint. Yet he fought the blackness closing in around him. He did not want his brother to see him cry. He was a grown man. It seemed like an eternity before a doctor came by again. Meanwhile Simon had drifted in and out of consciousness. The pain seemed unbearable.

"Hello, son. I'm Doctor Philip Turner. Doctor Tilton asked me to come and see what's going on with you." Turning to Jacob, "You must be the brother we have been looking for. Let's take a look here, shall we?" He lifted the dressing which lay over Simon's wound. "Oh, my," Dropping the dressing, he turned to Jacob, "Let's go outside and talk a bit."

Jacob followed Doctor Turner through endless rows of litters until they passed out of the tent into the rain. Fresh air filled Jacob's lungs, temporarily taking away his suffocatingly morbid thoughts.

"Your brother has suffered a serious injury. It could be life threatening. Fortunately his hip joint does not appear to be involved. It is too high up to attempt an amputation which we would not do in any case unless as a last resort. So we have to do what we can, and we have to do it promptly. I recommend that as much of the foreign matter as possible be removed.

Doctor Turner continued, "It is quite likely that fragments of cloth from his trousers have entered the wound site that along with any residual gun powder could cause infection later on. I think after we operate you should try to get him out of here and take him home if you can. Some of the men here have fevers and other infectious ailments that, in your brother's weakened condition, could complicate any recovery he might enjoy. I can have one of the mates talk with your commander to arrange a discharge for you so that you can take him home. You're from Middlesex County, aren't you? I think Mr. Hunt is in the same company, isn't he?"

"Yes, I'm from Groton, and my brother lives in Ashby. I'll get him there somehow."

"We have a number of other folks here whom I would also like to send home." Doctor Turner spoke with authority, "Perhaps you can all arrange to go together. If you go on the Post Road, I am sure you will find doctors along the way who can help you, change the dressing, and so forth. There may be others whose enlistments are about to expire who could go with you.

"I'll let you try to work that out for yourselves," his voice was gentle, "Sam Hartwell, our quartermaster can help you too. Now, you go do what you have to do, and I'll do what I need to do. I'll get a surgeon's mate, and we'll get to work. You don't need to spend any extra time in here with all the illness. Now run along. Give me a little while. Then go and find the pay master. You'll need some money for the trip. Try to gather up some horses, too. And God be with you. You will have an awesome responsibility."

With that Doctor Turner turned and headed back into the tent. It would have been first light by now if it were not still drizzling, but instead the sky was gray and overcast. It would be a cold, dreary day, another day without sleep.

Washington's main army was retreating toward North Castle while the British, instead of taking the offense, again procrastinated and waited for more reinforcements. Jacob, still in a state of disbelief at the rapidly unfolding events slumped under a tree and, leaning against it, put his head in his hands. I can't believe this is happening. What shall I do next?

Chapter XXII

PREPARING TO LEAVE

Again time stood still. How long Jacob had been sitting on the wet ground he did not know. His reverie was broken by the sound of a voice calling his name. He startled and looked up to see the friendly face of Private Paul Fletcher from Groton.

"Hey, Jacob! We're going home!"

"What do you mean," Jacob queried, "Are you going home too?"

"Yeah, a bunch of our fellows are sick. Hear Simon was hurt bad. They're sending Hinch Warren, me and you home with those who are sick and wounded. Our enlistments are about up. There aren't enough doctors. They can't take care of everyone so they are sending them out of here. Maybe we can get them as far as Stamford."

"I want to take Simon home. Doctor Turner is not sure he'll make it; and if he's going to die, I want it to be at home," Jacob, trying to keep his voice steady, was idly drawing circles in the wet ground with a stick as he spoke, not able to look directly at Paul for fear that he would see the terror and sadness in his soul and the tears in his eyes.

"We're going to need horses for the sick. They won't be able to walk that far. I think there are five or six who are sick including Simon. I guess we can double up if we have to. You and me and Warren can walk."

"Simon won't be able to ride a horse," Jacob said. "He is barely conscious. He was hit in the upper leg. They are going to try to get the bullet or whatever it is out, but they're not sure they can get it all. I am going to have to drag him somehow."

"Then we'll get a horse. You can ride the horse and drag Simon behind. We'll make a litter. It's going to be all right, Jacob. If we all work together, we will figure it out. All in all, we have been lucky. They say that the hill where we were yesterday is covered with dead Redcoats. We must have done something right."

Paul Fletcher was beginning to sense the depth of Jacob's despair. He placed his hand on Jacob's shoulder giving it a gentle squeeze as he stood to his feet. "You go see what you can do for Simon, and I'll find Hinch and round up some horses."

Paul Fletcher's familiar face lifted Jacob's spirits. He felt not so much alone. He could take a deep breath without feeling stifled. There was almost a spring in his stride as he walked over to the medical tent where Mr. Hunt was just finishing up with Simon.

Taking Jacob aside again he explained, "Jacob, the ball that hit Simon was pretty good sized, probably nearly an inch. Can't say for sure what kind it was, musket ball probably, but it did a lot of damage. Doctor Turner was able to remove the large pieces with his fingers; but when the ball hit the bone, it burst into particles; some of them are still in there.

Hunt proffered, "Just as a matter of information, surgeons prefer to remove bullets and other foreign matter with their fingers rather than with a probe because a musket wound will admit the finger easily, and it is not apt to catch on tendons or nerves. Feeling with the finger does not endanger the arteries, and the doctors can better judge the condition of the wound. They can follow the course of the ball and then either cut around it or follow it, and they will know whether it touches on an artery or a joint or whether it has broken any bone. In this case, the femur, that's the long leg bone, is probably shattered as well, but the doctor couldn't tell for sure. If the ball hit the femur, as he thinks it did, then the ball, in fragmenting, would tend to flatten out, broadening the area of damage."

Mr. Hunt used his hands to demonstrate his remarks. Jacob was beginning to feel a bit lightheaded, but he forced himself to concentrate on Mr. Hunt's eyes so as not to flinch. "Some of those foreign particles may work their way out later," Hunt continued, "Or your brother may need more surgery. There is likely going to be infection at the wound site. He's a little groggy right now. I gave him some spirits before the wound was probed, and I gave him a few drops of opium for the pain, so don't expect too much of him just yet. Try to keep his spirits up; and when he begins to come around, give him a little cider if he will take it." With that Mr. Hunt was gone.

"Simon. Simon. Can you hear me?" Jacob whispered, half hoping that Simon would remain asleep for a while longer. His eyelids fluttered, but there was no response.

Jacob sat by Simon's litter, occasionally stroking his arm.

His mind drifted back to their childhood days. He could remember their play together. He could remember visiting Grandfather and Grandmother Patch up on their farm. He could remember sitting in their cool kitchen in the summer and eating those warm, fresh, juicy blueberry pies that Grandmother made especially for them. He could remember going to school where they had learned to read and write.

So many memories. So many years have passed. There had been happy times, many happy times. He and Simon had been the closest of all the siblings as they were only two years apart in age. It was three years before Oliver had come along and another three years before Benjamin was born. The girls had come along later.

A kaleidoscope of images rolled through Jacob's mind. It wasn't until about ten years earlier that they had begun to drift apart. He had to admit he envied Simon his good looks and his beautiful wife. But let's put all that aside now. I must get him home. He's my brother. It is as if a part of me is lying on that bed.

It seemed as though hours had passed. Perhaps it was only minutes. No one could be sure. Jacob sensed that it was now mid-afternoon. Still Simon had not awakened. Jacob finally arose and went to the food wagon for warm cider and bread with cheese. It tasted so good. He saved a little cider in his mug and carried it back to the medical tent. By then, Simon was beginning to stir. Jacob placed his arm under Simon's neck, raising it a bit so he could lift the cider mug to his lips. A slight smile appeared on Simon's face as he felt the familiar warm aromatic liquid against his lips, and he swallowed. Thank you, God, thought Jacob.

"Simon, I'm here! We're going home! Paul Fletcher and Hinch Warren and I are being discharged to go home with you and several other of our boys who are sick. Everything is going to be all right. We're going home!"

* * *

The next day was also rainy, but Jacob was intent with purpose. He spent as much time as possible with Simon who was now conscious. His mind was more clear, and the pain was abating. His leg was still sore to the touch through the thick dressing, but the burning pain had lessened considerably. He was able to drink and eat a little bread. By tomorrow, he'll be able to handle a little meat, thought Jacob.

In between his frequent visits to Simon, Jacob had been to see Sam Hartwell, the quartermaster, who set aside three blankets for him. Jacob had explained that he would have to make a litter to transport Simon, and as he talked, a plan of action began to crystallize in his mind. He would find some oak saplings long enough to attach with vines to the girth holding the horse's saddle and long enough in the back to clear the rear of the horse with ease. He would then attach tree branches and a blanket joining the two saplings together. The blanket would support Simon's weight, and the horse would drag the makeshift litter and Simon.

Jacob admitted that he would not know until they set out how far they could get before the blanket wore through or the saplings broke from the weight. Another blanket would go on top of Simon for warmth, and Jacob would use the third one for himself. That was the plan. Sam Hartwell had told him to pick up the blankets just before they planned to leave.

Jacob had been waiting for the rain to ease up so he could locate the desperately needed oak saplings.

In the afternoon the rain became intermittent, and he headed for the nearby forest, taking his musket with him in the event he encountered a British sniper. After trudging through wet underbrush and mud, he came to a small group of oak. Lacking an ax with which to cut the saplings, he found a rock from a stonewall fence. Using the sharp side of the rock, he was able to sever the young saplings from their stumps. Paul Fletcher had located horses earlier in the day, and they were grazing contentedly under the watchful eyes of Paul and Hinch.

October 31st was another rainy day. It not only rained, but it poured all day. Everything not under a tent became soaked. It was also the day, the last day of October, that several men from Colonel Eleazer Brooks Regiment were mustered out, including the small band of sick and wounded from Middlesex County. And it was pay day. Those men who remained and were considered fit for duty were ordered to march and join in with George Washington's main army that had gone on ahead toward North Castle.

Jacob received his final instructions from Mr. Hunt. "Jacob, I think if the weather clears up a bit tomorrow, you had better head on out of here. Simon is stable at the moment although there is significant redness around the wound site. I am going to show it to you because you are going to have to take care of him as you travel."

They were standing beside Simon's litter; and as Mr. Hunt spoke, he demonstrated, speaking to both Simon and Jacob, "I've made a splint for him because his leg needs to remain as stationary as possible. As I explained before, the long bone may be fractured, and the splint will help keep it stable. The dressing we use is called an eighteen-tailed bandage which is really a thick pad, made by laying the bandage tails over each other with some folds of linen placed along the leg. I'm keeping the wound site wet using various solutions specifically for that purpose on the bandage. While you are traveling, you can use salt poultices or just water, if you have to; but for the first few days, you'll need to keep the bandage wet."

"I'm sorry to be so much trouble, Jacob," murmured Simon, "Can you do all this, Jacob? Can you get me out of here?"

"I'll do it, Simon. It will be done some how. I'm going to get you home. Together we can do it." Jacob was feeling a bit light headed, however. All this talk about sickness and wounds was making his stomach churn.

Mr. Hunt continued, "He seems to have a slight fever. You will have to monitor that too. He may have to be bled by someone along the way if his fever gets worse. I may give him a little mercury before the day is over. Along the way you can probably get someone to steep some bark tea for him." Noticing how pale Jacob had become, Mr. Hunt turned away from Simon's litter, "The dressing will have to be changed every day. I'll give you enough bandage material for a couple of days before you leave in the morning. After that you can probably find doctors in some of the towns who can help you. You are not that far from the medical facilities in Greenwich. Are you feeling all right?"

There had been little opportunity for conversation with Simon since the battle. He had often been sleeping or too drowsy to talk when Jacob had visited the medical tent; and remembering Doctor Turner's admonition, he had not lingered. On other occasions the few medical personnel in attendance discouraged long visits by Jacob.

Leaving the medical tent as quickly as he could, Jacob spent the rest of the day constructing the litter that he hoped would get Simon home to Groton. He gathered brush to place between the oak saplings, and tied them together with vines by weaving them in and out of the brush for reinforcement.

In the morning he would attach the blanket and then attach the litter to the horse. Let's see, what else do we need? We will need some food and beer and cider to start out with. We may need more ammunition in case we run into marauders or Tories who would do us harm. Surely we could use an ax in case there is a tree down on the road, maybe even a hunting knife. So much to do; so little time.

Chapter XXIII

HOMEWARD BOUND

Despite his exhaustion Jacob slept fitfully during the night . The rain thankfully stopped. There would be so much to do in the morning. His mind raced through a litany of worries, any one of them was serious enough to delay an early start. He tried to recall details of the march through Massachusetts and Connecticut, trying to remember the towns and how close together they were.

Where would we stay? Where would we find food? Could we get medical help? Would the litter work? Would the horse drag the litter without spooking? Would we run into loyalists? Would there be enemy scattered along the way? Would we be safe in Connecticut? How would we climb the hills and ford the streams? What would Father say when he learned about Simon? What about Elizabeth? The possible answers to that question were so painful, he awoke before daylight unable to sleep any longer.

During the evening while he was supping with Paul and Hinch, they had discussed the route they would take to reach the Post Road. There were two possible choices. The easiest route would be to travel south of Rye to meet the road that would only be about four miles from the New York-Connecticut line. It would only be a couple of miles from there to Horse Neck that they remembered was just south of Stamford.

The other possibility, a shorter route, would take them straight through the woods to connect up with the Post Road, but the terrain would be much more difficult. They decided to go by way of

Rye even though it was a few miles longer. At least they did not have to ford the Bronx River as they were already on its east side.

At first light Jacob woke Paul and Hinch. Paul rounded up the horses while Hinch gathered their muskets and went to collect a day's supply of food from the food wagon. Then Jacob went to the quartermaster to collect blankets before going to the medical tent. They had hoped to get a really early start, but that was not to happen. Sam Hartwell during the preceding two days had made inquiries and had determined that their trip through New York would be dangerous. They would have to travel very carefully. Tories were everywhere, and this caravan of sick and wounded could well be captured as prisoners or killed.

"You won't be safe until you get back to Horse Neck," Sam had said. "It may take you a couple of days to get there. When you get there, you need to go to Knapp's Tavern. It's owned by Captain Israel Knapp. They say that he is a Tory, but it will be a safe haven."

"Yes! I remember. We passed by there when we marched down from home," Jacob's face clouded as the impact of Sam's words began to resonate.

"Then you also know that there are other Tory hangouts in Connecticut, particularly in those southern parts." Sam continued, "Today though will be the most difficult one because you will not know who will be friendly and who will not. You will either have to camp in a field tonight or find a homestead friendly to our cause. There are some advantages to traveling as a group and some disadvantages. I think for you and Simon you will be better off traveling with others who can help you. If Simon were not so sick, you might be better off with two horses traveling by yourselves." Sam put his hands on Jacob's shoulders looking squarely into his eyes, "God be with you!"

Jacob, shaken by what he had heard, shared this new information with Paul and Hinch whose responses were light hearted and confident. For a brief moment Jacob felt relieved that he would be traveling with friends.

* * *

The previous day he had given considerable thought to the manner in which he would attach the litter to the horse, and he had attempted to select a horse from those available that in his judgment had the right temperament to drag a litter. Most of the horses were high spirited as would be necessary to perform in battle; but one of them, in particular, seemed a bit more responsive than the others to the human touch and voice. This is the one he wanted to take home. For the horse, the trip would be easy. He would be walking all the way. There would be no trotting, no loping and no galloping, but he would be responsible for the safe delivery of one injured soldier under harsh conditions.

Jacob also decided that by lengthening the stirrup straps on the English saddle to the lowest possible level, the litter would travel at a lower incline when the oak saplings were attached, making a more comfortable ride for Simon. Jacob would be able to vault onto the saddle without using stirrups as he often did at home when mounting an unsaddled horse.

At the medical tent he received final instructions from Mr. Hunt who showed Jacob again how to apply a fresh dressing and otherwise ready Simon for travel. Simon was experiencing more pain than he had the day before, and his fever was troublesome. Paul and Hinch would assume responsibility for the others who were sick.

* * *

The medical tent was in the process of being closed down. After discharge of the men traveling to Middlesex County, the rest of the sick would be transferred to the hospital at North Castle. By the time preparations for travel were complete, it was well past sun up.

Now, the next critical step would be to hitch the litter to the horse. Fortunately that was accomplished without mishap; but it required two people, one to hold the horse's head and the other to attach the oak saplings into the stirrups and lace them in with vines. Jacob hoped that when the horse became accustomed to his new role, this task would be a bit easier, and he would somehow be able to manage it by himself.

Thus, it was midmorning before Jacob and the small band of battle-worn soldiers were able to mount the horses they hoped would take them back home to Massachusetts. It had taken eleven days to reach Horse Neck; Jacob guessed it would take at least twice as long to travel the 200 miles home.

Although most of the British army was now located several miles to the west, the safety of the sick and wounded as they traveled would not be at all certain. Earlier in the morning the fog had been thick; but as it lifted, movements of the traveling band would be more difficult to conceal. Therefore, it was decided that those men traveling by foot would go quietly on about a quarter of a mile ahead of the horses to assure safe passage for Jacob and the sick. Paul Fletcher and Hinchman Warren led the little caravan of five sick men on horseback and Jacob and Simon out into the near wilderness.

The first day of travel proved to be singularly unpleasant and nonproductive. Would this be a harbinger of days to come, Jacob wondered. By necessity travel was slow. Jacob was having difficulty keeping the oak saplings in the stirrups, and he had to stop often to reattach them. Held together with brush and vines, the litter was not stable.

The blanket that lay beneath Simon dragged on the ground and would soon wear through, and Simon's condition appeared to be worsening. He was sweating. He appeared delirious, intermittently shouting, crying out and moaning as he was bumped along over rough road that had been badly rutted from the travel of many boots, horses and wagons. Simon's ride was anything but smooth.

Jacob's mood was solemn. What would Father do if he were here, he thought. How can I help Simon! It's such a long way home, but I have no choice but to keep going on. If I had left him back there with those overworked medical people, Simon would surely die. If I can get him home, he at least has a chance. What will Simon's life be like if Doctor Prescott has to amputate? I dare not think such thoughts, he reflected. I must get him some place where it is safe and where he can rest. The desperate need to move forward sustained him.

As the day wore on, the sick soldiers were also tiring. Paul, Hinch and Jacob decided among themselves that they would stop wherever they could before sundown. They would only travel about three or four miles this day.

"Do you think we should try to find a farm house?" asked Jacob.

"We've gone such a short way," responded Paul, "I'm afraid we might find Loyalists. We won't be able to fight off folks not sympathetic to our cause. We could be attacked. If we try to find farm people; and they see nine of us, not knowing that many are sick, they might do us harm. I think we should just camp in a field or in the woods tonight and then tomorrow try to make it to Horse Neck and Greenwich."

Purple shadows were beginning to stretch into the still emerald green fields like long fingers on a slender glove when Paul and Hinch stopped, allowing the others to catch up with them. Off to the right was an open field near a wooded area, and a small brook ran along its edge.

"I think this will do," offered Paul. It was a nearly perfect place to stop. No houses could be seen. A row of bushes and small saplings grew dense as a hedgerow along the road that would hide them from passersby although they had met no others on the road during the day. Everyone was hungry and tired. They had not eaten during the day, attempting to conserve what little food they had and not wanting to lose time by stopping any more than was necessary. Here they could rest and eat. The weather was still pleasantly warm. They would not be in danger of freezing although the night would be cold. By tomorrow hopefully they would reach more friendly territory.

They unsaddled the weary horses, allowing them to quench their thirst from the stream and graze in the open field. Paul, Jacob and Hinch were hungry, and they quickly devoured a meal of dried meat, bread, cheese and beer. The sick were all feverish, but with some encouragement they each consumed beer and bread, then huddled in their blankets and went to sleep.

Simon remained feverish. His dressing had been changed in the morning and would not require attention until the next day. He remembered what Mr. Hunt had told him about keeping the dressing wet. Cupping his hands to collect and to hold water from the stream, he applied as much water to the dressing as it would absorb, also dabbing water onto Simon's face, neck and arms. Simon wouldn't eat but did sip a small amount of beer. Jacob ate quickly as he needed to find more oak saplings before dusk turned to blackness, and he needed to repair the litter in preparation for the next day's travel.

Night fall comes more quickly as fall approaches; and without benefit of a fire or a full moon, everyone went to sleep after the sun dropped below the horizon of trees. Everyone slept fitfully. Jacob lay wrapped in his blanket beside Simon and listened to the erratic tempo of his brother's breathing. Simon's sleep was intermittent, and his arms flailed restlessly. I wonder what he is thinking, mused Jacob. We haven't had much conversation since he was injured. He's been too sick.

Jacob's thoughts turned to home for the first time since they had marched away. How strange it was not knowing what we were going to face. Now with each passing mile and with each passing hour, the daytime memories of the battle were beginning to recede from his memory. It's hard to believe that we are really going home. We aren't there yet though, and with that thought he dropped off to sleep. When he awoke, he really felt chilled. He reached over to touch Simon and found him awake and shivering.

"I'm cold," offered Simon.

Heavens to Betsey, thought Jacob as he jumped to his feet. "Here, Simon, I'm going to wrap you in my blanket for a while. Perhaps this will help," Jacob cried as he wrapped his blanket on top of Simon, up to his chin and under him as far as he could reach. The others one by one began to wake up.

The sky was still murky dark, but the horizon was beginning to brighten just above the tree line as it does just before the sun offers its orange new-day glow. It would be a clear, crisp day. Today they would some how travel all the way to Greenwich. It had previously been decided that Paul and Hinch would take the sick to the army camp at Horse Neck for the night before going on to the medical hospital in Stamford, and Jacob would take Simon to Knapp's Tavern as suggested by Sam Hartwell.

Jacob had proposed that Paul and Hinch, after leaving the sick at Stamford, take two of the horses and go on ahead to Groton. Upon their arrival they would first go to Ebenezer Patch's homestead and tell him about Simon and that Jacob would be bringing him there as soon as he could. Then they would visit Mary and help her in any way they could, assuring her of Jacob's safety. Lastly they would perform the most difficult task of all. They would go up to Ashby and tell Elizabeth about Simon.

With the plan of action established, they set out. Their safe passage the day before and the knowledge that they were close to the New York-Connecticut border gave them confidence in their ability to travel more safely. As Jacob rode along, he mused about the previously unthinkable possibility of Americans fighting Americans; this would occur if the loyalists fought with the British against the rebels.

It was around noon when Jacob, still struggling with the inadequately constructed litter, reluctantly told Paul and Hinch to take the sick and travel on ahead. "Simon and I will be there sometime today, but I don't want to hold all of you up. Your boys need to get medical care without waiting for us to catch up with you."

Jacob was on and off his horse all afternoon. Simon was becoming more feverish. He was barely conscious. He whimpered with pain as the litter was dragged over the many ruts on this well-worn road that had been so heavily traveled by troops and equipment. Occasionally, they met other travelers. Fortunately they were friendly, many of them offering to help. One farmer traveling with his oxen and wagon gave Jacob an old piece of rope.

"I've been carrying this with me for years in case of an emergency, or in case my harness breaks, but your emergency is greater than any I might run into," he said as he helped Jacob more tightly secure one of the oak saplings to the stirrup.

"Do you know of any doctors in Greenwich?" asked Jacob.

"Eyya. There are for sure. But if you're staying at Knapp's, you won't need no doctor. Captain Knapp's wife was married to a doctor once, and I believe she knows as much as any doctor in town. Looks like you're going to need her, too. Be on your way now. Don't waste any time. This brother of yours needs help."

Jacob thanked the farmer for his generosity and started out again. It was after dark by the time he and Simon finally came into Greenwich, crossing the bridge over the Byram River. How lovely this town appeared when we approached it just a few short weeks ago, Jacob thought.

He could still see in his mind's eye the brilliant panorama of crimson, gold and burnt orange covering the hills of Greenwich, and he remembered the expanse on the west side of the river sheltered by those giant rust-brown oaks. Greenwich, as he recalled, was on an elevated plain. Its hills were pristine and wooded. There were rocky dells, and its diverse coastlines were broken by deep harbors.

This evening it was too dark to see much beyond the road before him. He passed by several houses and crossed over Horse Neck Brook which as Jacob remembered led into the harbor. He also remembered that the Horse Neck Harbor area was largely pastureland, so unlike the rocky, hilly pastures at home. Shortly after crossing the brook was a church on the left and very soon up ahead Jacob could thankfully make out the faint lights of Knapp's Tavern.

"We are finally here," he said aloud, not certain Simon could hear him. He dragged the litter as close as he could to the door of the tavern. As he pushed the door open, he could hear voices, but inside were only a couple of people, regulars they appeared to be, talking with a short, stout, gray-haired man behind the bar.

The man behind the bar looked up with a sparkle in his eyes, "You must be the soldier with the wounded boy. I'm Capt'n Knapp," he said walking around the bar and coming to the door, "We've been waitin' for you. One of the lads from Groton came by earlier to let us know you were comin'. Where's that poor boy with the wound?"

Jacob stepped aside, taken aback by the friendliness of this caring stranger, and pointed to the horse. Captain Knapp grabbed a lantern from a hook on the wall and carried it out to the litter. "Well, now, let's just see here," he muttered to no one in particular while raising the lantern above his head for better visibility. Simon appeared to be sleeping, his face flushed and hot. "Oh, my, I'll get those chaps in there to help us get him inside."

Captain Knapp rushed to the tavern door, cracked it a bit and yelled, "Boys, put down your rum and give us a hand!" Turning back to Jacob, "I don't think we should try to get him upstairs yet. We can take him in through the tavern and put him on some blankets in that next room near the fireplace. I'll fetch Mrs. Knapp." He ran in through the tavern shouting, "Elizabeth! Elizabeth! Bring blankets. Hurry! Come on, boys, hurry up!"

Quickly, working together, the four men unstrapped Simon from the fragile litter and carried him in through the inviting tavern into the more formal front parlor, laying him gently on the broad-board pine floor near the roaring fire. Mrs. Knapp quickly appeared carrying an armful of blankets. Jacob was immediately struck by her motherly warmth. Her round, ruddy face, framed by a colorful, oversized bonnet, glowed in the light from the fire as she knelt on the floor beside Simon, her long skirts draping softly in the flickering light. With skilled hands, she felt his forehead and felt for a heart beat.

"Elizabeth, you know, was married to a doctor once, a Doctor Hungerford. She used to go with him on his rounds. Knows as much as any doctor, she does," offered the captain. His customers quietly retreated to the tavern. "What can I get you, my dear?" he asked his wife. Before she could reply, Jacob told her what he had been told by the medical personnel at White Plains about the dressing, the compresses and the fever. He told her that he had an extra dressing in his saddle bag and that it had not been changed since the morning on the day before.

"Well, go get it, lad, and we can take care of that straight away," she said. After Jacob left, she turned quietly to her husband, "It doesn't look good, Israel. This boy is right sick. It's a pity he has to travel so far. It'll put a real strain on his constitution."

Jacob quickly returned with the saddle bag, and Mrs. Knapp, kneeling on the floor beside Simon, removed the old bandage, "Oh, gracious!" she exclaimed. "That looks so sore. I know you are in pain. I'll be as careful as I can." She gently touched the red and inflamed area around the wound. "Not much that can be done now except replace the dressing and apply some compresses. Israel, go get me some hot water! Bring me some cold water, too!"

Simon winced as Mrs. Knapp worked. He was awake now, and Mrs. Knapp was talking to him softly, reassuring him that he was safe. She gently rolled him on one side to place blankets under him, being mindful of the splint holding his leg stable, and then carefully rolled him in the other direction to blanket the floor behind him on the other side. Finally, another blanket was used to make a pillow for under his head.

Mrs. Knapp covered the wound with hot water compresses and then made cold compresses for the back of his neck and his wrists.

"Israel, take this young man, Jacob, is it, to the tavern and feed him. There's lobster and bread on the table. Get him a pint of beer and bring one here to me for this lad," motioning to Simon.

Like other taverns of its time, the only public room was the kitchen which was like many other kitchens in the colonies except this one had a cupboard containing a variety bottles, mugs and glassware in one corner cordoned off by the bar. This room at Knapp's Tavern also had the usual assortment of fireplace hardware, toasters, long-handled shovels or peels used to remove loaves of bread from the Dutch oven, long-handled skillets for frying salt pork and a variety of three-legged kettles. A high-backed settle sat near the fireplace, and a few benches lined the walls. The bar patrons were no longer present, having gone out into the night and on their way.

Jacob wearily slumped onto the settle, watching Captain Knapp scurry about as he prepared a plate of food for him.

"I want to thank you for taking us in," began Jacob, "They told as at the medical camp that we should come here, and I want to pay you the going rate."

"Well, let's talk about that later. You had best think about staying with us another day or so. Looks like your brother needs my wife's attention," Captain Knapp paused, "I have a lot of sympathy for the cause of liberty, but I also still respect the Crown. It was back in '43 that I was commissioned Captain of the Training Band at Horse Neck. That was a long time ago. Then, of course, we were fighting the Indians, then the French. I never would have believed that one day we would be at war with our motherland, but here we are. I don't know about where you live, but there are a lot of Tories around here. Fact is, most families have got some," he continued wistfully.

"Captain, before I get too comfortable, I best take care of my horse. If it is all right with you, I will just unhook him from the litter and let him graze. He has probably already found the water trough."

"I expect he has. It's right under his nose!"

When Jacob returned, a plate of food was waiting from him and a pint of beer. Even though it was only early November, the warmth of the fire felt good after having spent the previous night out-of-doors. Jacob sensed that the good Captain had already had quite a bit of rum. He seemed to enjoy having Jacob to talk with, and he related to him about how he acquired his property, his family, his daughter, Amy, who still lived at home, about Mary and Hannah who were married and about his son, Israel, who served on the local Committee of Safety. Seems that Captain Knapp had purchased the tavern property more than thirty years previously and acquired his license to operate a tavern more then twenty years earlier.

He chortled, "I'm too old to go to war now. Much too old. Why, I'm way beyond seventy years. I've had a full life. Why, I was even a school teacher once. Then I became a shoemaker. All I can do now is run this tavern and help fellas like you and your brother once in a while and sit back and enjoy the respect others in our little village pay me."

Meanwhile, Mrs. Knapp was running back and forth from one room to the other.

"I think your brother is more comfortable now," she said, "He's sleeping, and I believe his fever is a bit better for the moment." Turning to Jacob, "If you want, you can sleep in one of the rooms upstairs, or you can sleep down here on some blankets near the fire."

"I'll just sleep down here near Simon and the fire." Jacob responded, "I don't want to put you out none."

"All right, then, I'll make up some blankets for you and make you a pillow, too, so you'll be comfortable. Captain Knapp and I will be sleeping in the room directly above you, so if in the night you need anything, you can just holler, and we'll hear you. Now I want you to stay with us tomorrow. You both can use the rest and nourishment."

The heat from the fire and the warm beer made Jacob feel very much at home. It reminded him of how he had felt last Thanksgiving at his father's house, silently recalling the pleasure and merriment of that occasion. He felt comfortably serene at this very moment, sitting here by the crackling fire with these two kindly souls. If only Simon were not so sick, he mused.

As he settled onto his billet for the night, after resurrecting the fire in the parlor with a couple of small logs, Jacob's thoughts drifted to home, to Mary, the children, his father and mother, and of course to Elizabeth. What would they say when they learned about Simon? He could still remember the sound of his father's words when he said that he couldn't get along without any of his boys. What would this do to him? He could hear Simon breathing in and out beside him, and soon he too drifted off to sleep.

During the night Simon alternated between shaking chills and drenching sweats, between hugging the blankets close to his body and then throwing them off completely. It was a restless night for both of them. Jacob was reluctant to disturb Mrs. Knapp, yet he didn't know what if anything he could do to ease his brother's discomfort. His own sleep was fitful, much like it had been for the past few nights. Occasionally in the blackness of this night he could still hear the bellowing of endless cannonade and the rat-atat-tat of field pieces and mortars. The imagery of men's legs, arms and bodies, mangled with cannon and grape shot, usually awakened him. He knew he was lucky to be alive.

* * *

The Knapps were up early the next morning. Their daughter, Amy, had not been seen the previous night as she never went near the tavern when it was open in the evening. She and her mother were busy in the summer kitchen in the back of the house when Jacob arose and joined them. They were making salt-meat broth and hasty pudding with molasses for Simon.

Jacob was perfectly content to remain in this comfortable household for one more day. Yesterday and the day before had been trying and difficult, and they had not traveled far, not more than six miles or so, he guessed. The litter had nearly broken apart.

The road around Rye had been merely an old Indian trail he recalled, and it was in that general area that they had picked up the more heavily traveled Post Road. They crossed Stoney Brook and a succession of necks and coves along the shore of the Sound. They passed through Saw Pit on the east side of Rye where they had seen a mill and boat building shop on the Bryan River near its mouth.

The trail crossed the stream at the wading place at the Great Stone where a fellow traveler helped them cross the water. But nothing had been as challenging as the terrain entering Horse Neck where a chain of rocks was so steep that if the horse had slipped, they would surely have gone down into a valley two or three hundred feet deep. Then they had come to an endlessly long hill before reaching the Tavern on flat land after dark. Jacob had stopped frequently to make adjustments and to stabilize Simon's position on the litter. How I wish there were some other way, he thought.

After breakfast Jacob stepped outdoors into a bright, sunny and crisply cool autumn day, the kind of day reminiscent of those earlier halcyon days at home when he was just glad to be alive. A wooded area encroached on one side of the house where spent leaves were still raining down with each puffy gust of wind.

The house sat back from the road and was built in the style of the day, except that the front door was oddly off center, unlike most of the newer structures. In fact he had often thought that all carpenters seem to follow the same general plan of construction. When it came to the fronts of houses, they all had a classic design with an artist's attention to balance and scale. When it came to the ends of houses, each carpenter seemed to follow his own instincts, and in most cases, house ends lacked the symmetry and elegance characteristic of the fronts. But this house was oddly different because of the placement of the front door.

Jacob rounded up his horse. Captain Knapp had told him the previous night that Greenwich, because of its proximity to the border with New York, was a hotbed of Tory activity. "The Tories are as thick as patriots," he had said, "It's a no-man's land." The lawless elements or bushwhackers were known as "skinners" and would move in and take advantage whenever a chance for pillage arose. This explained why he and Simon had not met any of the town's folk on the road. This horse, rider and wounded soldier were vulnerable to attack, and Jacob made a mental note to travel only during daylight and to take shelter somewhere when darkness descended, at least until they reached Massachusetts.

During the morning Jacob collected more oak saplings and decided to use two of the smaller ones as cross pieces between the saplings that attached to the stirrups. This would hold the saplings together, and he would secure them with wooden pegs. Young sucker growth was collected as well to fortify the area between the saplings and create a cushion for Simon to lie upon. While he worked, he absentmindedly wondered what the next few days would bring.

By the time Jacob returned to the house, tavern activities were in full swing. It was Sunday, and the tavern was busy even before church services began. The tavern was close to the Episcopal church, and Jacob surmised that Captain Knapp's customers were more than likely parishioners who were loyal to the Church of England rather than members of a Congregational church or other denomination frequented by the rebels.

During the day, the tavern was a place for the exchange of news of the day, and Jacob knew that after services were over, the tavern would fill up again as the conversation turned to other, more philosophical matters. He could hear Captain Knapp's voice above all the rest, and he could picture his rosy, smiling face and his shoulder-length white hair dancing on his shoulders as he moved from one customer to another filling the pewter mugs with rum, cider, beer or wine according to the pleasure of each man.

Jacob entered the front door as he did not wish to intrude on the tavern regulars. The parlor where he and Simon had bedded down was filled with chatter as Amy and Mrs. Knapp cared for Simon. A pile of clothes covered a nearby chair. Mrs. Knapp was changing Simon's dressing while Amy was coaxing him to drink the broth she had prepared for him earlier.

"I am so grateful to you for all you are doing for us," offered Jacob.

"Well, you are more than welcome, I am sure. Simon seems to be about the same as he was last night. The wound is about the same. I am only changing the inner layers of the bandage, leaving the outer layers for protection. I know you will want to leave early in the morning, so you will need to get the dressing changed somewhere tomorrow. Perhaps you can go to the hospital in Stamford."

Mrs. Knapp continued to murmur comforting words to Simon as she worked and talked with Jacob at the same time. She nodded her head in the direction of the clothes' draped chair. "Amy and I found some things that we want you to take with you. The clothes you are both wearing are badly worn and spattered with mud; and if you get wet fording a stream, you will need something dry to put on. Some of these things belonged to the captain before he put on weight, and others belonged to one of our sons."

"I don't know what to say," murmured Jacob softly, "There is no way I can repay you. I already owe you so much. I may not have enough money for the rest of the trip!"

"Oh, we're not charging you, Jacob," Mrs. Knapp replied turning to face him. "We've talked about it. Captain Knapp has been honored to hold a tavern license, and we are grateful for that privilege. These are trying times. The captain is too old to fight on either side, but we both want to do something to support our people through this time of terrible trial, and at our age being able to help you lads makes us feel useful. Now," she paused shifting her ample weight slightly, "you will need to help me change Simon's clothes. Amy, go get some cold rags. We need to work on this boy's fever!"

During the afternoon Jacob worked diligently to mend and rebuild the litter for travel. His fears were eased after talking with Mrs. Knapp as he had been fretting about his mounting tavern and lodging bill. Mrs. Knapp's extraordinary generosity relieved his anxiety, and his confidence returned. He would get Simon home. Some how he would.

Chapter XIV

STAMFORD

Jacob awoke at the break of dawn the next morning. At Mrs. Knapp's insistence he had bunked upstairs during the night, and he felt remarkably refreshed. This was the first night in more than forty when he had been able to sleep soundly and comfortably, and he was less haunted by the demons of war. With the lifting of early morning fog, this day promised to be as nice as the one before, and Jacob was anxious to begin the trek.

Simon seemed a bit worse this morning. He still had spikes of fever despite Mrs. Knapp's best efforts. He felt weak. Sweating was profuse. He was unable to eat. He complained of persistent headache, and his wounded leg felt as though it were on fire. His usual sunny, optimistic disposition had turned to despair. All he wanted was to be relieved of pain and to get home as quickly as possible.

Mrs. Knapp prepared a bag of meal for each of them. An entire meal in a bag, it contained salted fish, cheese, bread and roasted turnips. They could either eat the food cold or heat it when they reached an inn or a tavern. They were also supplied with beer.

Captain Knapp helped Jacob move Simon to the litter, and together they strapped him in and wrapped blankets around him. Their destination would be Stamford. They would be traveling into Tory country where many of the inhabitants had already taken up arms for the British or who had letters of protection because of their allegiance to the King. Jacob felt anxious but prepared.

Leaving Greenwich the Post Road descended from the high land and went by way of Dumpling Pond over the narrow bridge spanning Miamus River, then through the low land area bordering the river. Traversing over the river on that finger-thin bridge was heart-stopping, and Jacob dismounted from the horse, leading him over as any sudden movement might have tipped the litter over into the amorphous, swirling water below.

Magnificent granite bluffs continued to hug the coastline as they traveled east along the ridge. Deep harbors broke through the coastline. They continued for about six miles over road little better than what they had experienced earlier. They skirted boulders, rocks, bogs, inlets and navigable streams, finally arriving on the exquisite tree-lined green of Stamford late in the afternoon.

Simon's condition had worsened during the day, and Jacob's first thought was to reach the hospital. He could easily understand why the military had chosen this strategic location for a hospital. Located between two hills, Palmer's Hill and Richmond Hill, on the west and Noroton Hill on the east, the area was more secure than Greenwich was further to the west.

Jacob had never seen an army hospital before, and he knew that this one was a branch of the hospital in North Castle. Makeshift, at best, he thought. Unlike the army military tent at the White Plains camp, this facility was located in a long shed-like structure with rows and rows of men lying on bed ticks, coarse linen sacks filled with straw to form a mattress. Some of the sick and injured were lying directly on piles of straw covered with what appeared to be the soldiers' own blankets. All rested directly on the ground.

These men must be those who were injured or discharged as sick from the New York campaigns, he thought. There were far more men here than had been wounded at White Plains. Understaffing was a problem, and he waited for an eternity before he finally grabbed the attention of a surgeon's mate.

"Don't come in here," the mate warned, "I'll come to you," as he herded Jacob away from the open door. "What can I do for you?"

"It's my brother. He was injured at White Plains, and we've been sent home to Massachusetts. We have a long, long ways to go, but he is sick something terrible."

"You've been discharged, hey?"

"Yes, that's right," responded Jacob.

"Well, I'm not sure what I can do for you. We are what is known as a regional hospital. We treat those men who have not been admitted to a general hospital. These men haven't been discharged from the army yet. We have to account for everything, each meal, each man treated, every dose of medicine. We have nothing to spare. No extra food and certainly no extra bandages or medicine." The mate paused, shaking his head in despair, "You would probably be better off in a private house or inn. But let me take a look at him."

As the mate spoke, he stooped down to the cool ground beside Simon's primitive litter. He could quickly see that Simon was in considerable pain. His heart was pounding, beating rapidly under the experienced fingers of this medical officer. Simon was sweating profusely. Without even examining the wound, the mate concluded, "He is in what we call the hectic. His body is trying to heal itself. He probably can't eat. He looks thin and wasted. What we are looking at here is a process, the inevitable aftermath of injury, about what we would expect to see a few days after such a wound."

He rose to face Jacob, "Doctors here have to report to the deputy director general who supervises the hospitals in the north and east of the Hudson River. We aren't able to get all the things we need from the general hospital. Any soldier with special needs such as anyone who cannot eat his regular rations just doesn't get fed unless we can acquire such items locally, and that is very difficult, particularly at this time of year.

"We need Indian meal, oatmeal, rice, barley, molasses and wine among other things," he continued, "This is the kind of diet folks like your brother should have, but we just can't get enough! It's so sad. We lose men every day because we cannot provide what they need." The young mate pushed a strand of light brown hair back from his face, "Look, I tell you what I am going to try to do for you. I am going to try to get him a few drops of opium. That will ease his discomfort a bit and let him sleep. And perhaps I can find a bit of linen to place under the dressing, but that's about all I can do. And don't come inside! We've got smallpox and dysentery in here."

When the mate came back, Jacob asked, "Do you know where we can find shelter for the night?"

Shaking his head and not looking up as he worked on Simon's bandage, the mate offered, "You are just going to have to take your chances. I don't know this town very well. I only know there are lots of Tories here. There are also lots of taverns, but I don't know anything about them. I never get to leave this place." When he lifted up the bandage, Jacob could see that the area around the wound was fiery red and puffy with fluid; the surrounding skin, turning blue. He turned his head away, feeling suddenly dizzy. He had killed animals, and he had dressed them. He had seen raw flesh before, but this was his brother. It could have been his own flesh.

"Just be cautious when you approach a tavern and listen to the voices," the mate proffered. "You will be able to tell whether the tavern customers are friendly or not if you listen to their words. Try to pick a place where there is a barn where you can sleep. The hay will keep you both warm. Get some wine. Perhaps you can get your brother to take some. It will ease his pain some."

Jacob's concern abated somewhat after the mate told him that Simon's condition was following an expected progression. Perhaps things may not as bad as they seem, he thought. I should have inquired whether there were any lads from Groton at the hospital. By now Jacob was back out on the road, and his thoughts quickly turned to more immediate needs. It had been an uncommonly pleasant fall day, a bit on the cool side, but lovely nonetheless. It would soon be pitch dark. He continued slowly east. Each step along the road took them both closer to home.

In Stamford he encountered more people on the road than at any time since leaving the army camp, mostly old men and a few young boys, all trying to hurry home before darkness rolled in with the mist from the sea. In the distance an old man was walking by himself. He used a walking stick and appeared to be lame. As they approached one another, their eyes met, and a look of understanding passed between them.

"Howdy, son," the old man spoke. "Traveling through, are ye?"

"Yes, sir. We're coming back from White Plains and going home to Massachusetts," Jacob tilting his head toward the litter to include Simon.

The old man, now seeing the man on the litter for the first time, "Is he sick?"

"No, but he was wounded in action at Chatterton Hill the end of October."

"Looks like you could use some help. What can I do for you. Wish I could have been there with you. I'm so mad at those daggone Brits and what they're puttin' us through I could spit nails!"

"We need a place to spend the night. Any ideas?"

"Sure do. I've got a barn where you can bunk down and feed your horse. You won't want to leave him out of doors during the night around here. Not safe," bending over to inspect more closely the unusual method of transportation, "Looks like this bedding needs a little fixin' too."

The two men continued chatting as the old man whose name was Joseph slowly led the way to his house. Jacob breathed a sign of relief. Finding a place to stay for the night proved much easier than he had feared. I wish I didn't worry so, he thought. I wish I could be more like Simon, more carefree.

Reaching the barn, Joseph swung the great barn door open as it creaked on its giant iron hinges. Jacob breathed deeply, quickly taking in the smell of newly gathered hay. A wave of nostalgia broke over him, and in his mind at that brief moment he was back home in his own barn. How he wished he were there now! He judged this barn to be a good one. Must be nearly fifty feet long, big enough to support this old man and his family. Probably not planning to enlarge his farm so he doesn't need anything bigger.

Eager to be of assistance, Joseph suggested that the litter might be made stronger by attaching something to join the saplings together in addition to the oak cross pieces.

"Ey, ya! I've got just the thing! There's an old sail from my old boat around here somewhere. You can have that, and we can use some rawhide straps to lace it onto your saplings. Two men, younger than me of course," he chuckled, "could carry your brother if you need to ford a stream. You will be able to carry him anywhere as easy as can be.

"Young man," he continued, "I caught fish before I had a sail boat. Now, if we don't win this thing, I won't ever need another sail boat!" He paused. "You'll have some weather before you get him home. This sail will make it easier. May God travel with you."

After making Simon as comfortable as possible on a stack of hay, Jacob who had not eaten during the day, took a break and ate some of the cold food Mrs. Knapp had given him. Joseph shared his wine with Jacob and Simon, and the two men began working on the litter. The sail was big enough so they could lay it double thickness between the oak saplings, giving Simon additional support.

While they worked, they talked, opining politic and speculating on the future of the new republic. Jacob was in better spirits than he had been in several days. He was certain now that they would somehow get home without mishap. He was asleep by the time he hit the hay that night and did not stir until the gentle sounds of his horse woke him at daybreak.

The opium was beginning to wear off, and Simon was becoming restless again. Jacob gave him the rest of the wine left over from the previous night. Knowing the terrain would be rugged and challenging for a few more days until the road turned north, he was anxious to start as early as possible. The status of the litter was greatly improved, and Jacob hoped he would be able to travel further each day and stop less frequently. At least that was his plan.

Chapter XXV

GROTON

Little news was reaching Groton these days. The talk around town was that the Americans had retreated from New York to some place north of the city. This was of little comfort to Ebenezer who now had three sons in the army. New England militia had somehow been assimilated into the Continental Army. In addition to Jacob and Simon, Oliver had also enlisted. The whereabouts of his sons were unknown. Benjamin was the only one who was still at home to help around the farm; and because he was so busy, trips to town were made only as a matter of necessity and not merely for social reasons.

Not only had Benjamin worked with Ebenezer at home but had gone up to Jacob's to help out there as well. Whenever he had any spare time, which was seldom, he rode up to Ashby to check on Elizabeth. As soon as one or more of his brothers came home, he would reenlist himself. Fortunately, the needs of the Patch family were few as no money was coming in; and, like other farm families, their accounts around town continued to mount. Taxes were rising to help support the war, and there was concern among many townsfolk that they might face imprisonment if they could not pay them. Farmers wanted protection from imprisonment until a currency was established and trade resumed.

Hearts were heavy during these days. There was no way of predicting how long the war would last. With the exodus of the British from Boston, fear for one's personal and physical safety had been replaced by fear of economic hardship. Inflammatory writings roused people to resist imposition of laws. Ebenezer in addition was worried about the safety of his lads. Not one of those from Groton inducted into service at the end of September had been heard from in nearly six weeks.

One rumor Benjamin and Ebenezer had heard that they found particularly offensive concerned the wearing apparel of the militia that had apparently been criticized as the men were not wearing standardized uniforms. Some of the Connecticut regiments, those from New Haven for example, wore sky blue coats with red facing while the Massachusetts militia wore homespun clothes. Farmers went to war with the same clothes they had been wearing while plowing in the fields, clothes that had been sewn by their women folk out of cloth spun and woven in their own kitchens.

It was even more distressing to hear that their Commander-in-Chief, George Washington, had also bemoaned the appearance of his troops. Both Benjamin and Ebenezer felt that the Americans might have already lost the war if these same farmers had not been able to respond so quickly to the call to arms. Why, the British might still be in Boston, they thought, or even in Groton by now.

There had even been talk of removing the lead weights from the meeting house windows and melting them down into bullets for the town stock! As economic hardships mounted, so did the level of underlying unrest and down right fear. A general sense of foreboding prevailed.

Chapter XXVI

STAMFORD TO
NEW HAVEN

After leaving the agricultural town of Stamford, Jacob with Simon attached securely to the litter headed east. Fortunately, fine, cool, clear weather accompanied them. The roads now were crude and poorly maintained. Ridges rising 500 feet ran north and south along the banks the Rippowam River. The landscape was wooded and hilly with outcropping stony crags.

That night they bunked in a barn behind the Connecticut House in Norwalk which was located at the lower end of town where the sea vessels anchor. The Connecticut House was an austere, three-story building with a cupola on the roof and a row of pillars in front.

Jacob was mastering the daily routine now and was less worried about Simon after talking with the surgeon's mate in the army hospital. The litter was holding up well, thanks to the kindness of the old man in Stamford. He stopped at a store along the way to pick up food, and he purchased wine and beer from a tavern. Simon's condition was no better and perhaps slightly worse, but, Jacob thought, that is to be expected. They traveled ten miles that day.

The next morning they again started early. Heavy blue-gray fog had dropped down during the night, enveloping everything with its clammy dampness. A chill in the air reminded Jacob of the lateness of the season. Visibility was so poor that it was like walking through a cloud accidentally fallen from yon high. In fact each morning had been foggy; but by midday when the fog lifted, the sun broke through as if a new day was finally only now beginning. The wetness vanished like it had never existed at all. It is amazing, thought Jacob, how one's mood follows the weather. In the mornings I feel sad; but when the sun comes out, I feel restored, and I'm certain that we can endure these trying times.

At the east end of Norwalk they passed a series of mills, stores and two churches and climbed a steep hill to the town green, boasting a smattering of trees and several houses. After passing out of the town, the road made a number of unexpected turns on its way to the Saugatuck River. Jacob had been warned about the Peat Swamp, and they approached that area with great caution as it was known as a haven for criminals, men who would not hesitate to rob, or worse, and had been known to attack post riders.

Beyond the Peat Swamp was the tavern of Major Ozias Marvin. Jacob remembered this tavern from when the company had marched south. Today he stopped to let his horse drink from the trough in front of the tavern. There was much raucous activity, and several horses were tied up in the front. Half a dozen children were hooting and hollering. They appeared to range in age from about five to thirteen, and they seemed to be enjoying this spectacular fall day, gazing intently at Jacob and his odd-looking carriage. Jacob was growing accustomed to the impolite and pitying stares of people along the way, and he tried to ignore their halfhearted curiosity.

About a mile and one-half beyond the tavern they came to a river. The Saugatuck was navigable for a greater distance than any other stream in the area. The lowest fordable place was two and one-half miles from its mouth, and Jacob had to travel the extra distance along the banks to the upper bridge that spanned the river where they could cross over.

After a long and challenging day, they finally arrived at Green's Farms. Jacob had forgotten how beautiful this particular stretch of land was. Earlier they had marched through too quickly to appreciate its splendor. Bounded on the north by the Post Road and on the south by the Sound, this fertile land gently rolled out toward the sea. It was a virtual plantation, and off in the distance stood a handsome white church.

Vapor could be seen rising from the grassy salt marshes. What a sight that was. Despite the difficulties of travel, this had been a beautiful day. It was even warmer than usual, and reflections from the setting burnt orange sun could be seen bouncing off the water in the distance. How I wish Simon were well enough to enjoy this, he thought, as he slowed his horse to take in the vista before moving on.

They spent the night at Passel's or, rather, in the barn at Passel's. Because of Simon's fever, the surgeon's mate in Stamford had suggested that tavern owners might be reluctant to take them in because of fear of disease being carried from the army camp. Jacob had no objection. He was just as happy sleeping in the barn as it reminded him of home. Dragging the litter into a barn was much easier than attempting to move Simon into a house and up one or more flights of stairs. It was also less expensive. In fact so far they had not been charged for sleeping in barns, only for horse feed and the wine and food they bought from the tavern. Jacob wanted to take home as much money as possible.

Breezes picked up during the night, and by morning a steady cool wind was blowing off the water. Jacob was reminded that it was November, and winter weather would likely be encountered soon, long before they reached home. In the morning they continued to follow what appeared to be old Indian Trails.

The barkeep at Passel's had told Jacob that this trail, known as Pequot Road, would take them all the way to Fairfield. A mere bridle path, it followed the ocean, winding in and out. Later in the day as they approached Fairfield, hundreds of acres of salt marsh were visible inland to the right of the trail and bordering the water. The road converged at the village green with other paths coming from several other directions. Beyond the houses surrounding the green was a cluster of common fields where visages of earlier crops remained, where cattle grazed, and where new homesteads were being built to accommodate the town's growing population. It appeared to be a prosperous town.

The serene harbor was filled with sturdy sea worthy vessels as well as fishing boats. Jacob speculated that in better days this town would have traded with Boston and New York and even as far away as the West Indies. All up and down the coast could be seen whaleboats. Jacob had been told that the whaleboat men had been busy attacking British vessels in the Sound. In fact, they also had made raids on the Tories on Long Island. True patriots, they were.

The Sun Tavern was located opposite the green and was owned by Samuel and Elizabeth Penfield. The house was a large colonial with three floors. Five windows on each of the first two floors faced the green. The third floor had three windows on the front. There were large double chimneys on the roof and a full front porch. There late in the afternoon activity was in full swing. People were milling about. A few horses were tethered. Others were grazing on the green. Children were playing. Jacob sensed the warmth of this place and decided to stop, hoping to find accommodations.

A young man was bustling about behind the bar. Jacob approached him, explaining that he had been a soldier at White Plains. His brother, also a soldier, had been wounded, and they were traveling home to Massachusetts. The young man went out to the litter and saw that Simon was uncomfortable and sweating. It would have been impossible to carry him in that condition up one or two flights of stairs to a room which he would probably have had to share with one or more other people. The young man, whom Jacob assumed was one of Mr. Penfield's children, offered accommodations in their shed which fortunately contained some straw that they could form into a pile for sleeping.

As Jacob and the young man stepped up onto the porch again, one of the younger Penfield children ran into the house,

"Mother, mother! There's a wounded soldier going to sleep in our shed! Come quickly!"

Mrs. Penfield responded at once and offered assistance for which Jacob was extremely grateful. He explained that he needed linen in order to freshen Simon's bandage, and he would need to buy some food and beer or wine. Other than that, their needs would be few. In response to Jacob's question, Mrs. Penfield told them that she would try to find something appropriate for Simon to eat.

Simon seemed worse, Jacob thought. He still had fever and sweats. He wouldn't eat; and when Jacob changed the dressing that night, the wound was becoming more swollen and extremely painful. The skin was increasingly blue. Sometimes Simon would respond when Jacob tried to talk with him, and other times he would not. He seemed asleep.

That night Jacob went into the tavern for the evening meal that was served at a long pine table, much like his mother had in her kitchen. Everyone ate together. It was the first home-cooked food he had had since they left Knapp's Tavern. He knew that in a few days the road would turn north, and he wouldn't have access to as much if any fresh fish that was so abundant here along the coastline.

During the night a strong gale from the ocean brought with it a chilling fog; and by the time they started out the next day, the wind had turned, coming now from the northeast. They would be heading into it, now making travel much more arduous. But they had to keep moving on.

The road, still following old Indian trails, wove in and out and about in an irregular fashion until they reached the Pequonnock River at the head of the tidewater. No bridge existed over the deep stream at this point, and it would not be fordable until they traveled inland some distance from the sound to a bridge. Just before crossing over the bridge was the store of Philip Nichols where Jacob stopped to let his horse drink and to purchase bread, cheese and salted fish.

Jacob sat down under one of the giant trees nearby to rest and to eat. Again it was not possible to encourage Simon to eat more than a mouthful of bread and drink a little beer. A short distance beyond the bridge the Post Road passed through Old Mill Green and beyond to enter Stratford at the mouth of the Housatonic River.

Harpin's Tavern, earlier known as the Pixley House, was located at the intersection of the Post Road and another road. The green here was wider than most and extended into the Sound itself. The clapboard tavern was surrounded by trees and had a center chimney and full front porch. A school house also stood on the green opposite the milestone. An Episcopal church appeared to be closed. Stratford was quiet and rural compared with the towns they had recently passed through. Jacob decided to stay at Harpin's for the night and cross the Stratford River by daylight.

A chilling northeast wind continued throughout the night and into the next morning when Jacob and Simon set out after breakfast. A flatboat ferry took them over the river. There were a couple of taverns nearby, and after traveling about three miles, according to the milestones, they came to the Milford town center. They passed on the left a large rock known as Hog Rock. The winding road turned north and came into the town at the First Congregational Church. The elm-shaded green was at least one-half mile in length surrounded by several homes, some of them taverns. Because of inclement weather and Simon's weakened condition, Jacob elected reluctantly to spend the night in Milford.

The next day, the road to New Haven turned left in Milford. West Rock soon came into sight. Jacob remembered this landmark from his march south. This abrupt cliff resembling lava sheets appeared to continue north as a long ridge. The road followed the Old Milford Path, going up over the summit of Milford Hill. They then crossed the West River at the old West Bridge, traveling through the wide marsh to the west of New Haven, and after about a mile and one-half they finally arrived at the green.

Jacob remembered this as being an especially densely populated town. Even though darkness was now descending, he could see that hundreds of homesteads surrounded this vast green; nearly twenty acres in size would be a good guess. There were three churches, a court house, jail, stocks, whipping post and pillory. Surely, there must be a doctor in this town, Jacob thought. Simon desperately needed something for pain. The spirits Jacob had been giving him were no longer keeping him comfortable. He needed help.

Chapter XXVII

NEW HAVEN

Jacob stopped at the first tavern he came to, the house of Mr. Beers. It had been a excruciating couple of days. Nearly half a day had been spent traveling inland to ford the river, requiring much more travel and distance than would have been necessary otherwise. Perhaps they could spend the night here. He was tired. Simon was moaning in pain and probably wouldn't sleep tonight any way, he thought.

Listening to his story, the barkeep told him, "You'd best see Doctor Hubbard first thing in the morning. He's on the green, easy to find. He's held in very high esteem in these parts. Don't try to see him tonight though. They entertain a lot in the evenings, important folks, you know; but he is always in his surgery in the morning."

The young girl behind the bar turned away. Jacob could hear bottles clanging together as though she were looking for something. She finally reappeared with a cracked pewter mug and filled it to the brim. "We have little rum these days, but here's enough to quell his pain for the night. You come back later and sup with us, hear?"

The next morning following the directions he had been given, Jacob found the grand and elegant corner home belonging to Doctor Leverett Hubbard, and, as expected, he was in his surgery. Doctor Hubbard was a large man; his complexion, ruddy. His lips were thin, and his eyes were piercing and extremely dark. On his head he wore a white wig. This man is surely a pillar of society, thought Jacob, who had never before seen such opulence.

Together they were able to carry Simon into the surgery where he was placed on a table in the middle of the floor. Simon was sweating profusely and shivering from chills. Doctor Hubbard carefully removed the dressing from Simon's leg. Jacob turned his head away in horror. The sight was unbearable. The leg had become badly swollen and was beet red. The shiny skin looked as though it would burst.

Speaking softly to Simon, "Son, I am going to have to lance this wound and let out the malodorous fluid. That will relieve some of the pressure you are feeling. First, a few drops of opium to help with the pain." Doctor Hubbard rose and opened a closet in a corner of the room near the fireplace.

The closet was filled with small glass bottles, green ones, blue ones, brown ones and clear ones, each containing a stopper, some glass, others cork. Jacob was astonished. He didn't think that Doctor Prescott could possibly have such an array of medicines.

After administering the opium, Doctor Hubbard took Jacob by the arm and they went out onto the porch. "Jacob, is it?" Jacob nodded silently. "Why don't you wait out here while I work on your brother. My wife can help me, and I'll speak with you after I've finished."

With that the doctor went back into his surgery, and in a few minutes Jacob could hear the swishing sound of silk. That would be Mrs. Hubbard joining her husband in the surgery. Soon Jacob could hear Simon's screams, and then silence was punctuated by agonized groans as he bit down on the bullet Mrs. Hubbard had placed between his teeth. The doctor went about the business of gently pushing on the tissue around the wound while extracting a large quantity of thick yellow pus mixed with blood. The exudate contained particles from the tissue walls and was tinged with gray and yellow fibers.

"This is about as bad a wound as I have ever seen," he muttered to no one in particular.

For Jacob, those agonizing moments passed slowly. It seemed like an eternity before the doctor joined him on the porch, leaving his wife to minister to Simon. "Jacob, your brother's wound is filled with the most grievous material I have ever seen," Doctor Hubbard sat down beside Jacob on one of the benches that lined the front walls of the square, hammered-stone house and wiped his brow. "A lot of this material has been removed, but it will continue to drain for several days. He is a mighty sick lad. I guess you know that. I told him that amputation might become necessary, but he is adamantly opposed to the procedure, and in his case it would be particularly risky. It is only performed as a last resort, when nothing else can be done to save the life of the patient."

"Will he be all right?" Jacob asked. "He has a family, three small children and a new baby."

"Well, I hope so, but there is no way to be sure, you know. He is in the hands of the All Mighty. I am hoping that by relieving this pressure that has been on him, it will enable him to begin to heal. If that happens he should be all right, but it is really too soon to tell."

It would have been an unlikely sight to a passerby to see these two men of such different backgrounds sitting side by side on the porch of this elegant home, the aristocrat and the yeoman. They sat silently now, each lost in his own thoughts. Occasionally, they would speak, but mostly there was silence, broken only by the sounds from inside the house, the hustle and bustle of a busy household, and folks passing by on the street. Servants appeared to be scurrying to and fro. Children were reveling in the carefree joy of just being together in the safety of their intimate surroundings.

Jacob was tired. He had just traveled over some of the most difficult terrain imaginable under the most trying of circumstances.

Finally Doctor Hubbard appeared to have gathered his thoughts and suggested to Jacob that he allow Simon to remain in the surgery for the day. "The Provincial Congress has recently voted that towns along this road be required to establish hospitals staffed with doctors where soldiers returning from battle can be cared for and can receive refreshments. Looks like I am starting already!" Doctor Hubbard told Jacob. He would be nearby in case Simon needed something, and his proximity would allow him to monitor the patient's progress. Jacob breathed a sigh of relief, not having any idea how to care for someone as sick as Simon seemed. Jacob needed time to restore the litter before moving on.

* * *

The town of New Haven was built on a large plain, remarkable with its immense green. Fewer than 400 houses existed with the main settlement on the edge of the harbor. Although very large, the green was unkempt and unfenced. The ground was marred by wagon ruts and a new growth of bushes. Livestock, geese, swine and cattle, grazed uncaringly and contentedly in the gentle sea breezes wafting off the water.

Most of the houses were constructed of wood. The better ones were painted blue or lead color; the majority were red. The houses displayed courtyards in front decorated with trees and shrubs of various types. In the back were gardens containing fruit trees and the residual of vegetable gardens recently harvested. The public buildings, including the State House and the newly constructed meeting house, were brick. Behind the meeting house was the ancient burying ground, crowded and neglected and surrounded by a crude wooden fence painted red. There were three college build-ings. It was a sleepy town perhaps due to the war.

Jacob knew that he should spend time repairing the litter for Simon, but he couldn't bring himself to work today. His mood was contemplative. His life was changing, and he had no control over his future. The war would alter our lives forever, and the future was uncertain at best, he mused. What if Simon failed to survive? What would happen to Elizabeth and the children. How would I be able to help? I have my own family. My family. I have not thought of them for days. Why not? What is wrong with me?

* * *

He found himself in the main part of town close to the water. He had felt compelled to walk in this direction. The smell of salt air and fish was intoxicating. Soon he would be headed northward away from the magnificent ocean. The terrain would eventually become completely different and more similar to home, more fa-miliar. A blanket of wispy fog was lifting slowly, leaving a veil of haze hovering lightly over the buildings. This day would be cloudy, but on other days when the earth was shrouded in sunshine, warm light would be filtering through the haze by now. Feels like rain, he thought.

The air was incredibly cool and damp, clutching him as though in a chilly but comfortable cocoon. Yes, comfort is what he needed right now. Gentle waves lapped against the narrow, sandy beach. Occasionally a larger, more urgent wave roared and crashed against the rocks, breaking into thousands of tiny white droplets that re-joined the retreating wave, only to return again and again, time without end. Jacob sat down on the wharf and took note of the many boats lying in the harbor, each with its own story to tell.

The wind was picking up, causing the boats to dip and sway to the rhythm of the waves. Jacob allowed himself to become mesmerized by his surroundings so different from home.

A few fishing boats had already left the harbor for the day, a hazardous business with a war going on, Jacob thought. At the end of the wharf a boat was being loaded with supplies that, he speculated, hopefully might be going to our troops. Mostly elderly men were idly standing around, men who during better times would have been actively engaged in fishing or transporting goods for trade with Boston or New York. Without work, there is no money, Jacob knew all too well. Again, he was overwhelmed by a wave of uncertainty, almost to the point of despair. He wished Simon were himself. Simon was always the cheerful, optimistic one. He could always be relied upon to say something good about the country's state of affairs in general and about their own lives in particular.

Without the sun, Jacob had no idea of the time of day. Gray storm clouds were rolling in from the sea bringing with them a bevy of screeching gulls that hovered near the shore in search of food. All of a sudden he too felt hungry. Somewhat restored, yet still numb in spirit, Jacob silently bade the powerful ocean adieu and walked slowly back to the tavern. He would work on the litter in the afternoon. He would replace the oak striplings and reverse the position of the sail in order to distribute the wear more evenly.

* * *

The next day black storm clouds dumped their cargo of rain onto the town, not a good travel day to be sure. Simon's condition was improved. He was awake and alert. His eyes twinkled and a broad smile brightened his slender face when Jacob entered Doctor Hubbard's surgery. Jacob's spirits soared, and he breathed a deep and thankful sigh of relief. Simon's fever was down, and the wound continued to drain. They would leave in the morning.

"It's so good to feel better," Simon offered, "How can I ever repay you and Doctor Hubbard for all you have done for me?" Addressing Jacob, "Doctor Hubbard's son, Nathaniel, has been a big help, too. He wants to become a doctor like his father and grandfather."

"No need, son," Doctor Hubbard said. "It's just what one soldier would do for another. I am also in the army, you know. I'm an officer, but it seems I can be of more value staying here at home and taking care of you boys as you travel through than I can by serving in a battlefield hospital!"

All of a sudden Jacob was ready to move on as soon as the rain abated. The feelings of anxiety and emptiness he had been experiencing were gone. Simon's smile had restored his emotional equilibrium. Home beckoned.

Chapter XXVIII

NORTHWARD BOUND

"Here we go," Jacob commented to no one in particular as he coaxed his horse to move on out. It was Tuesday, November 12 when Jacob and Simon finally left New Haven and headed north on Neck Lane. They had been on the road for eleven days, and to Jacob it seemed like a vast eternity. But now they were finally on their way home.

The drenching rain had slowed to a drizzle during the night; and although still gusty, the day was suitable for travel. The air was cool and damp still, and low clouds hung thick and close to the ground. Jacob would have liked to have started out earlier, but Doctor Hubbard insisted that Simon have something to eat and be properly wrapped with warm blankets.

As Jacob had anticipated, the road heading inland represented an improvement over the nearly impassable paths experienced south of New Haven. Although much narrower now than in earlier times, the road had been heavily traveled but was now muddy from the previous day's heavy rain. Folks in the towns north of New Haven were not able to rely upon sailing on the sound to facilitate trade and thus were forced to depend upon the highways for all travel.

Jacob and Simon followed the old winding Indian trail, crossing the Mill River by bridge. On the left, East Rock towered overhead, majestic even on this cloudy, dreary day, and on the right were reed-filled meadows bordering the Quinnipiac River. They passed through the river valley on level ground. This lush valley and vast meadows to the east would likely offer up bountiful hunting, they speculated. Beneath the meadows were deposits of clay, making North Haven a town for brick manufacture. They passed mills where small seafaring craft were built, and they arrived in North Haven in late afternoon. Darkness was arriving earlier with each passing day. This day proved to be the very best since leaving White Plains.

Doctor Hubbard had suggested that they stay for the night at the tavern of Gideon Todd for whom he had great respect. They called him "Gid". According to Doctor Hubbard, Gideon Todd had created a sensation in colonial society when he married Prudence Tuttle of Wallingford. The Tuttles, according to the story were wealthy aristocrats, and although Gideon Todd was their equal by birth and lineage, he had yet to make his fortune and so was not considered an appropriate marriage candidate for their beloved Prudence.

Nonetheless, Gid and Prudence eloped, and Prudence was disowned by her parents. When they were first married, they slept on a straw bed, and through the years Gid accumulated property and garnered the esteem of his friends and acquaintances. One day Prudence's parents, wishing to make amends to their son-in-law, came to visit bringing with them a cart full of gifts and provisions. When they arrived at the Todd's home, they were told by Gid that although they were welcome, their gifts were not.

Gideon Todd became known as a man of great energy and decision. Until the Boston tea party he had been a supporter of the King, but subsequent to that event he became a supporter of the cause of liberty and had earlier served in the military. It was in his barn behind The Rising Sun Tavern on Northford Pike that Simon and Jacob spent the night, sleeping soundly in yet another pile of newly gathered sweetly aromatic hay.

The next day dawned warm and sunny. It would be another good day.

Chapter XXIX

THE COURIER

It was about mid afternoon on a blustery day with no sun, a typical monochromatic November day in New England. Ebenezer wasn't sure of the time. The days were much shorter now than during the summer months, and he knew that soon nighttime would engulf the homestead.

He was in the barn baiting the animals when he heard footfalls in the distance. Probably just someone passing by, he thought, but as the sounds of galloping hoof beats came closer, his curiosity was aroused. Opening the walk-through door on the front of the barn, he saw a figure on horseback coming closer. A stranger, it was. A man. Yes, it was a man riding fast. He was bearded and disheveled, his long hair streaming behind. Who can that be? Doesn't look like anyone from town.

The rider pulled the horse up short as he neared the barn. "Ebenezer Patch!" the rider exclaimed breathlessly. "You don't recognize me, I know, I'm Paul Fletcher."

"Oh, yes! I do know you. Paul, of course," Ebenezer paused to collect his thoughts. Paul Fletcher was the last person he would have expected to arrive on his door step. Why, I thought Paul Fletcher had gone with Colonel Brooks Company when Simon and Jacob left in September, he thought. "What are you doing here? Have you come home?"

"Slow down, Ebenezer, let me tell it." Paul jumped down from the horse, allowing the reins to trail on the ground. He bent over at the waist to stretch his legs and then leaned backward to ease the strain on his back. "Whew! Hinchman Warren and I just got back from White Plains. We were in the battle there. What I came to tell you is about Simon and Jacob. We were all in the battle together. Jacob is fine, but Simon . . .," Paul dropped his eyes to the ground, and he kicked an invisible stone, unable to meet the gaze of the older man. Ebenezer's penetrating blue eyes were unflinching. "Simon was hurt! Hit in the leg by a mortar, he was."

If Ebenezer had not been leaning against a pitchfork, he surely would have teetered. "What happened," he said softly.

"I'm not really sure how it happened. All I know is we were stationed on one of them hills. It was a last minute sort of thing. We had no defenses to speak of. The other hills were well fortified, but ours wasn't. . .There were so many of them. They just kept coming. It was horrible. I can still hear the roar of them cannons. I'll never forget it! We had to retreat back to our camp. Jacob found Simon later that night in the medical tent. He had been picked up in the field. He was in pretty bad shape. The doctor tried to remove the mortar fragments. He was discharged a day or so later with the rest of us. They sent Hinch and me home with the sick and wounded. We've been traveling for about twelve days."

"Where are they? Where are my lads?" Ebenezer's voice rose to a frantic pitch.

"We had a bad storm come through right after the battle. We couldn't travel until the heavy rain let up. A number of local boys were discharged all at one time. Eight, I think from Townsend, John Gilson from Pepperell and about seven of us from Groton."

"Where is everybody?"

"Well, they are mostly sick, except for Hinch and me, that is. The doctors didn't want to take them to the hospital in North Castle where the army retreated. They thought it would be best to send them home. The hospital was understaffed, and there was more disease in the hospital than there was outside of it. So we were all discharged. We found some horses that the British had left behind. Simon was not able to ride a horse so Jacob made a rig for him out of oak saplings so he could drag him home behind a horse. It was slow going for him. That first day we didn't get very far at all. Jacob told us to go on ahead so as not to slow us up in getting the sick home, and I promised him I would come and let you know what happened as soon as I got back. I haven't even been home yet. I came here first."

Ebenezer shook his head in disbelief. "I just can't believe it," he murmured softly. What will we do! What will we do, he thought.

"Tim Warren from Townsend was sent home with the sick too. After a couple of days on the road, we decided that the sick should be checked by the doctors at the army hospital in Stamford to be sure they could all still travel. If any of them couldn't travel any further, they could stay there at the hospital, and the others could come on home with Tim Warren. Hinch and I decided to come ahead to let you and Elizabeth know about Simon. I don't know what else to say."

"Paul, you did the right thing. I'll send Benjamin over to talk with Elizabeth," Ebenezer offered.

"No need, Ebenezer. Hinch is going home to Townsend anyway. He is going by way of Ashby and will stop at her place on the way."

Neither men spoke for a few moments. Ebenezer had so many questions. He wanted to know everything, but he knew Paul was anxious to get home and probably didn't want to speak of the war any more for a while. How long will it take for Jacob and Simon to get here? What had the battle been like? Will we win this thing called liberty?

"I expect Tim Warren will probably be along in a couple of days with his group of sick. Tomorrow I plan to go see the Gregg's; both John and Samuel are sick. So is Benjamin Fisk. His folks will want to know too."

"How long do you think it will be before Jacob gets Simon home?"

"I don't know, Ebenezer, it could be weeks. The travel is real tough and dangerous. There are loyalists in those southern parts who won't help any and perhaps even British snipers."

"Paul, perhaps Benjamin and I should go and try to meet them."

"No, I don't think so. It would be too easy to miss them if either of you take a wrong turn or go off the road for any reason. It would be best if you stay here and get ready for their arrival." Paul bent down to pick up the reins, "I had best get on home now. My little boy is just over a year old now, and Thankful doesn't know I am coming, of course." He was mounted now, "Ebenezer, if there is anything I can do to help out, send Benjamin for me. I'm sorry to bring you such bad news, but they are alive! Can't say the same for all those Redcoats we took down! A lot of our boys have been lost too. After all that we've seen, thanks be to God for any tokens of goodness."

Ebenezer watched as Paul Fletcher rode down the road toward home. The tears welling up in his eyes were now streaming down his face. There were no sobs, just tears that he could no longer hold back. A sense of despair and disbelief swept over him, crushing his thoughts into numbness. Paul disappeared out of sight. Had his visit been real, or had it been a bad dream? It was real, he know, but there had been a surreal quality to it. He slowly finished those chores that were necessary, leaving everything else for another day.

Both Sarah and Benjamin were in the kitchen when Ebenezer entered the house, "Ebenezer, what is it? Are you sick?" asked Sarah.

"It's Simon. He's been wounded," catching Sarah as she fell into his arms.

* * *

The next morning Benjamin rode over to Ashby to see Elizabeth. She saw him coming toward the house and opened the door for him. He was horrified by her changed appearance. She had grown painfully thin; her beautiful delicate features were more chiseled now from exposure to weather that had transformed her clear porcelain skin into a bronze roughness. Clearly she had been working in the fields during harvest time. Her eyes were red and swollen, and she looked as though she had not been sleeping. She was uncharacteristically unkempt in appearance. Her clothes were wrinkled and splashed with mud that had dried into a brown, gray film. Her hands were calloused, red and roughened.

"Oh, Benjamin," she cried, throwing her arms around his neck, "What am I do do?"

In the fall of the year Ashby, Massachusetts, was usually the most glorious place on earth. Those were the sentiments Simon had always expressed at this time of year as he went about the fall chores. This year was different. Cardinal red leaves from the maples had already shriveled into purple and died. The yellows and oranges of the ash and beech trees were slowly wafting down to earth to join the fallen reds, baring graceful branches in the waning fall light. Days were becoming shorter, and a chill in the air reminded Elizabeth of the coming winter.

A decision had been made. Aunt Elizabeth would be leaving soon to go back home. She was tired and anxious to return home before snow fall. Elizabeth and the children would go to Groton and stay with Ebenezer and Sarah until Simon came home and was well enough to return to Ashby. There would be plenty of room. Benjamin would double up with some of the younger children, and Elizabeth and her children would take the other large bedroom in the front of the house. Benjamin and Ebenezer would bring the animals down to Groton, and the Ashby house would be closed up, probably for the entire winter.

It was with great sadness that Elizabeth had come to this decision. She had known right along that Aunt Elizabeth would be leaving when the weather turned. Although it had been a God-sent having her here to share the burdens of daily life and the worries about the future, there was a finality to it all. Aunt Elizabeth was aging and probably would not live to see too many more winters.

The passage of time and the changing seasons in the world of natural surroundings was one thing, but to think about it in terms of human cycles was entirely different. Elizabeth felt uncomfortable thinking about such things. There had been so much sorrow within the family already that Elizabeth did not like thinking about one day losing Aunt Elizabeth too.

Despite the generational differences, they had developed a close bond during the weeks they had shared together. But there would be no way that Elizabeth could cope with the farm, the children and the animals during the winter by herself. Benjamin had been the one to convince her that she should spend the winter in Groton, and Elizabeth knew there was no other reasonable choice.

Leaving the home she and Simon had created would be heart breaking. The thought of walking out the front door and closing those memories behind was at the moment unthinkable. It would feel like a chapter ending in her life, she thought, as she went about her chores, and she had to constantly remind herself that she would only be away for a few days or a few weeks, and then life would return to normal. Or would it?

Chapter XXX

THE GOOD DAYS

The weather could not have been better when Jacob and Simon left North Haven on Wednesday morning, November 13th. It was one of those rare November days when it feels more like spring than autumn. The air was balmy, and the sun was warm enough to heat the body through and through. A thin white layer of frost had blanketed the ground during the night and still glistened in the light of daybreak, giving way during the early morning hours and leaving the rich, dark soil moist and malleable.

Spirits were high. The Todd's hospitality and assistance had been most welcome. The tavern had been full, both with troops heading home and troops heading south into battle. The bar had been lively. Jacob, busy caring for Simon's needs, did not participate in tavern activities but, rather, was comforted by Simon's sense of well-being and optimism.

After dressing the wound with Mrs. Todd's assistance, Jacob retreated to the barn with two cups of hot cider and settled down in the hay at Simon's side where they talked and joked, seemingly erasing the tension that had from time to time kept them apart, enjoying the warmth of the hay around them and the sedating effects of the cider. They reminisced about times past being careful to avoid certain romantic topics, and for the first time began to talk about returning home. Simon's desire to become a trader and merchant burned deeply in his soul, and his dreams expanded as he talked of the limitless possibilities that would be available to him when he recovered.

Jacob was jubilant. Simon's optimism was infectious, and they both felt confident that their futures would brighten. The week beginning November 11th was shaping up to be a good one. Simon was finally improving. Drainage from his wound continued. To Jacob that was a wonderful turn of events. Simon's fever was down. The weather was moderate with sun-filled days and pleasant daytime temperatures. Only one day had been blustery, and they spent that night in Amos Hall's tavern in Wallingford. It was not until the 21st of November when they reached Suffield that the skies began to fill with dark, ominous rain clouds signaling the onset of fall rains.

During this period the folks along the way had been helpful. Tavern keepers allowed them to sleep in barns and provided them with food and drink at modest prices. As they traveled further north, their concern about confrontations with Tories began to subside. They felt safer. With each passing day home was becoming closer. Anticipation was mounting, tempered by the fact that there were many miles yet to travel, and they were still in Connecticut. This they remembered was tobacco country. They were in the lush, fertile Connecticut River valley.

They had not as yet reached the Massachusetts line although they knew they were very close. In fact some had said that Suffield had been once part of Massachusetts until a few years ago when it had become part of Connecticut. They had traveled more than fifty miles in the past ten days, not bad at all. But with the weather closing in on them, Jacob knew that it was time to ease up a bit and prepare for what would be the difficult trek across the western Massachusetts wilderness. Suffield would be a friendly place. There were few Tories there, he had been told, and most people were loyal to the cause.

Chapter XXXI

MASSACHUSETTS

Two days before they arrived in Suffield Simon began to complain of tenderness in his leg just below the knee. They were referred to Dr. Neil McLean in Wetherfield who corroborated Jacob's worse fears and advised them to move on to Suffield before the rains came. Jacob's heart sank. His mind went back over the many conversations he had had with doctors along the way who had warned him of the seriousness of Simon's wound.

In Suffield they were referred to Doctor Alexander King whose office was in his home on Main Street. The home was a fine colonial structure in a heavily wooded area, featuring a center chimney and a covered porch at one end behind which was the doctor's ample office. As soon as Doctor King saw the wound, his facial expression told Jacob the bad news.

"Son, I think you have an infection in the bone," his voice softened as he gently laid the dressing back over the open wound. He beckoned for Jacob to follow him from the office to the kitchen where he could talk without being overhead by Simon who lay on a table in the office.

"As sure as there are stars in heaven, I'm sorry to have to tell you this. But your brother is a very sick lad. His infection is deep inside. There is considerable pus in there, and he is experiencing great pain." Jacob inhaled in a long gasp and stared speechlessly at the doctor, who continued sadly, "The only thing we can do is to keep him here in our bourning room for a few days to see how he does by staying quiet. My wife can tend to him. We will keep him as comfortable as possible. We will give him some opium. I know you are anxious to get him home, but I'm not sure he will make it. You have a long, tough journey ahead of you. You must be prepared for many hardships."

A wave of black despair engulfed Jacob as the gentle doctor led him down the porch steps. The "not sure he will make it" phase hung on the air like moisture on a humid, hot summer day. I have to get him home, thought Jacob; I just have to. What will people say if he doesn't make it home. It will all be my fault. They will remember my feelings for Elizabeth and think I had reason to fail in my mission to get Simon home. The brains of a goose, they will say and worse.

Torrential rain fell for four days. Mud filled the deeply rutted paths in the common that Jacob judged was at least thirty rods wide. The weather was too miserable for travel even if Simon had been able, and Jacob used the time to rest and to take care of needs not attended to when they were on the move each day.

Jacob was morose. He visited with Simon every day. He did not seem to be improving. Jacob fretted. Simon was conscious but in great pain. He remained feverish. Despite the heroic efforts of Mrs. King to encourage him to eat, Simon's only desire was to get out-of-bed and continue on his journey home despite his debilitated condition. At times he was not coherent, and that new symptom only added to Jacob's malcontent and sense of desperation. The trip thus far had been slow and painstakingly methodical, but because of Simon's worsening condition, Jacob's inherent plodding nature was being replaced by a new sense of urgency. Additionally winter is coming on quickly, he mused, and travel conditions will be worsening with each passing day.

They had arrived in Suffield on a Thursday; and it was not until the following Tuesday that the skies cleared, and the sun came out. Jacob could put off their departure no longer even though the roads would be barely passable in places, and so it was that on the 26th of November they departed for West Springfield where they hoped to stay at the tavern on Elm Street. Simon will have to be as tough as a boiled owl to withstand the tortures of this trip, thought Jacob, as his now faithful horse lumbered along, dragging the nearly prostrate body of his brother northward and eastward.

Leaving the lush valley of the Connecticut, they crossed the state border into Massachusetts and into the village of Agawan. The land there was divided into three parallel strips according to its distance from the Connecticut River. The alluvial meadows bordering the river were known as the "plain lands." The next strip was called the "inner commons" and the farthest from the river, the "outer commons".

It was in the "outer commons" band where the terrain would become rugged and treacherous. Northward from Suffield the Post Road was bounded on the west by the southern end of the Holyoke range of hills. Fortunately, a ferry provided the means to cross the river where the road began to head east, ascending the hill to the plain at Springfield and continuing on until it reached the Chicopee River.

The descent from the plain was hilly, rocky and steep, and it was again raining. Jacob's heart was breaking as he tried to cross streams and remove fallen trees from the road. The ruts in the road were deep from wear and now filled with rain. There were slippery boulders in the path, threatening to rip the litter into tiny pieces, but they pushed onward. There was no other way.

The horse frequently slipped on the buildup of wet leaves hidden beneath the newly fallen rain, lurching the litter violently from side to side With each jolt Simon cried out in pain, and Jacob wondered how much more he could bear. The Bliss Tavern was in

Wilbrahan. We must get there. We just must. Finally, on the night of November 28, they reached the tavern and remained there for two days until again the weather cleared enough for travel.

Saturday the 30th proved to be another miserable day. The weather was cold with intermittent rain and snow flurries; but they set out again, and after half a day of travel the Post Road entered Palmer and hill country, heading for Walker's Tavern in Palmer Old Centre. In Palmer they crossed the Chicopee River. This was largely agricultural land with farms and homesteads nestled in the river valleys, but the road carried them also up over rough and rugged foothills.

Their next destination was Weston and then on to Brookfield. Traversing the hills took all the stamina and forbearance Jacob could muster; but once they came down on the eastern side of the foothills, the road became more passable albeit muddy. And yet the rain continued. The land was cultivated, and the road paralleled the Quaboag River which it followed through Brookfield where they put up at the newly constructed Hitchcock tavern.

During the march to White Plains both Jacob and Simon had been fascinated by the environment around them, the changing landscape, the configuration of the towns, the activities of the people as they went about their daily chores, so similar yet so different from home. This time it was so different. Jacob remained totally focused on the task at hand. The days began to run together, punctuated only by the ups and downs of Simon's condition and the need to take care of him as best he could. Jacob intuitively knew this was a race against time. With each passing day the urgency to reach home became greater.

Jacob lost tract of the number of doctors they had seen and the number of home remedies doting women had concocted in an attempt to alleviate some of Simon's distress to no avail. Jacob knew that Simon was not improving. In fact as each day passed his condition seemed to deteriorate. As he thought back over the experiences of the past few days, it became clear in his own mind that considerable disagreement had existed among the opinions of the various doctors who had treated Simon.

One had said that some fragments from the penetrating body probably still remained in the recesses of the tissue of his leg. Another had recommended amputation and was highly critical that the military personnel failed to offer that remedy as an alternative. Collectively, they were surprised that Simon was allowed to travel home. They seemed to have neither the recognition of the horrors that existed in a battle field military installation nor any understanding of the dangers to the patients who remained there. They certainly did not understand about the shortage of trained hospital people or about the pernicious lack of medicine and supplies.

Despite those admonitions Jacob was glad they had been allowed to leave. In his reverie he could still hear the screams of dying men; he could still see bleeding bandages hastily thrown over open wounds through which he could only imagine the seepage of guts or brain matter.

These men would just lie there until overwhelmed by the blackness of death while the medical staff busily tried to stem bleeding from reparable wounds, severing arms and legs in the process, in the all too often vain attempt to save lives. During those moments of retrospection, tears would stream down his face, and he would turn his head away so that Simon could not see. At least my brother is alive, he thought, and his determination to deliver him home to his family became even more etched in his psyche.

They forded unknown numbers of brooks and streams. They were wet more often than they were dry. Folks had given them clothing, blankets and food and sent them on their way again.

Women had ripped up old clothing to make bandages and placed cold compresses on Simon's forehead to relieve the fever. They had boiled bark and forced it down Simon's parched throat until he could take no more.

The sail that had been given them by the old man at the beginning of the trip remained barely intact. It had worn through in places where it dragged along the ground when the saplings and other vegetative supports wore out. Jacob could no longer even remember that kindly old man's name. It seemed an eternity ago. Neither could he remember the names of all the other wonderful people who had helped them. It was becoming just a blur, an uncomfortable dream that would not go away. Day after day.

The only change was in the weather. Like Simon's condition it continued to deteriorate. After another rainy spell that ocurred around the first part of December as they traveled through Weston and Brookfield to Spencer, Simon began to complain about his other leg. His leg was swelling and was turning red. It's getting colder, thought Jacob, and beginning to look like snow. We must hurry. If only someone could come to meet us. We are still several days from home. In fact, they did not arrive in Groton until December 10th, fourteen days after crossing the border separating Connecticut and Massachusetts and only two days before this year's day of Thanksgiving.

Chapter XXXII

REFLECTIONS

Doctor Oliver Prescott mounted his horse where it waited at the front door of Ebenezer Patch's house and headed for home at the usual slow, steady gallop. This horse, the doctor's favorite, had learned to take all possible rests while awaiting his rider's return from visiting a patient, knowing he would be expected to reach the next stop in the shortest possible time.

Today was different. As soon as they topped the rise west of the house out of sight of the homestead at a point just beyond the fork of the road that turns left toward Mr. Tyng's sawmill, the doctor drew his mount down to a walk.

"Whoa, now, hoss, take it easy. I have got to do some thinking about this case. That boy fails visibly every day in spite of everything I have tried to do for him. I remember that after he had been home for a couple of days he talked, during one of his lucid moments, about wanting to hobble out doors to look about, but now he couldn't if he wanted to, and I certainly wouldn't let him. The proverbial optimist, that one!

Straight ahead past the schoolhouse, old hoss, this road to the left goes down across the brook and just past Ben Hazen's, Jacob's wife's folks, you know. Just keep walking along. It may be that this boy will die. If he does, it will because of exposure from that long, miserable trip home. And thinking of that, what poor Jacob must have gone through getting Simon home. A crushing responsibility for anyone, but in this case it was his own brother and gravely wounded at that.

Jacob must have suffered as much as Simon but in a different way. One suffered unbearable physical torture, and the other, mental anguish. I'm surprised Simon has lived this long. If only I could have seen him the day after the battle, he would not be this condition. Jacob had said, "All the doctors tried everything."

I must talk to Jacob about that again, thought Oliver. Probably every farmer's wife and every would-be doctor from here to New York prescribed every nostrum ever known to man, and they probably made up a few new ones. Best of intentions, trying to help out, of course. I must keep trying and never let anyone know that for one moment I have any doubt of the outcome.

The wound in his leg is badly infected, but there is more. His other leg may have been frostbitten. I saw sweat standing out on his skin as I listened to his heart, and he asked his mother to stir up the fire. More digitalis, must increase the dose tomorrow. His heart is weak one moment, and the next, strong. Beats erratically. There is pressure of some kind inside his chest. He is having trouble breathing. His skin is blue, and he has a rasping cough. Why? The family is taking turns watching over him day and night. I feel helpless.

"That's it. There is one thing I can do. I will plan to spend more time tomorrow, and I'll have a talk with him if he is able. If not, he will hear the sound of my voice. I will talk of his future and the future of the colonies and in this way try to build up in him a greater desire to live. Sometimes that does wonders when all the feeble efforts of a physician fail. The boy does have a good future. I know about some of his plans. Elizabeth told me that first night he was home when I stayed with him so late. I will include her in this. With both of us discoursing on good days close at hand and the eventual success to follow, a miracle may happen; and that is what we need about now.

I've known this boy all his life. He's a worker, strong and ambitious with a beautiful wife and four fine children. Why is he in a fix like this. I wonder, really now why it is so? Don't be a fool, Prescott. He answered your call to the militia as well as the other boys did, Jacob and all the others. How many Massachusetts boys went on the White Plains campaign? Ah, yes, nine companies, 627 men. Well, now how about Samuel Gilson from Pepperell, and there was Henry Fletcher of Chelmsford. They went too, and the return read, "Killed in Battle."

There were others too, Now, those who are now in the Great Beyond, do they blame me? I doubt it. There was no other way. They knew it as well as I did. There is nothing for any of us to do but fight until we win. Perhaps we all fall into the niche planned for us, and it is my damnable lot to see these boys sacrifice; and it's their lot to sacrifice and regrettably to be sacrificed.

We must preserve liberty to make the most of our own lives as best we can. That's the right of every American and of every Englishman too, only they won't fight for it. We have felt this way for hundreds of years, way back to that day at Runnymede. We must think of those who will come after us.

What if I have to make another call to arms? It was only a few months past, July of this year, of course, that Mr. Jefferson's Declaration was read from the State House in Boston, and I remember the closing phrase, "We mutually pledge to each other our lives, our fortunes and our sacred honor." There it is right there. Probably I will have to make several more calls before we win this thing. I will do it if necessary, and we will win. We must, and then we shall be free men. It's the right of every human being!

Back to the business at hand. What would Doctor Robey do in this case if he were here? He taught me almost all I know about medicine. He would come back in the morning and find out about the pressure in Simon's chest, and that is what I am going to do. Try harder. Never stop trying.

I 'll talk with them, and I will take a look at Ebenezer too. I noticed today that he looked pretty peaked. Is the shock and strain of all this beginning to drag him down? Ah, could it be? Could it be camp fever? Is it possible the boys brought it from camp or maybe a slight case of typhoid? Could they have had it about them all the time since leaving White Plains? I think it very possible. Ebenezer is no doubt weakened by strain and possibly taken with the fever. I have done everything I can think of, but I must try harder.

What does every believer do after he has done what he thinks is his best. Ask for help from the Creator of all mankind. Oh, God in Heaven help me to do even more than my share in this frightful way. Steady my hand, sharpen my brain. Show me the way to save this life from being lost in the cause of liberty. Simon is a young and true soldier. We need him, and his family needs him. As I sleep this night touch me with the gift of wisdom and touch him with the gift of life. Thank, thee, Father of us all. Amen.

What was that? A shout? Ah, now, it's Will Dalrymple tearing out of his front door, shouting and waving his arms. He is in trouble and needs help. "Whoa, hoss, whoa!"

Chapter XXXIII

ETERNAL PEACE

On the morning of December 31, 1776, Jacob Patch raked over the few live coals remaining from the dying fire, and, sitting down on a low bench by the hearth, he carefully laid small split slivers of dry white pine one at a time on the graying coals. The early morning sky outside showed only the faintest glimmer of light in the east. Sunrise would come soon. Stars still shed their cold and mysterious winter light, and against this background the tops of great pines against the clear sky outlined Jacob's clearing.

His thoughts were not on the work of the dawning day but were of Simon. The battle was nearly two months ago now. They had been home only about two weeks. Thanksgiving this year had been subdued and solemn, so unlike the festive occasion of last year, now just a distant memory.

As he watched the steadily growing flame, a few snapping sparks and a thin spiral of smoke vanished above the lug pole. Recent events unreeled through Jacob's mind as they had done so many times in the past. Images of the long march to New York were beginning to fade from his memory. Warm thoughts of his family of young children and his good wife, Mary, whom he had left behind as he had marched away, had sustained him until the battle.

As it always has been to soldiers, the battle itself was a thing apart, a time when the past slips away and the present takes front stage. Only fragmented glimpses of a hoped-for future remain in one's focus. But the trip home with Simon was the reason for his restless sleep. Anxieties that he would never be able to put into words were still deeply imbedded.

What if he had not succeeded in getting Simon home? Those sly gossips would recall that it was he and not Simon who had first courted the fair Elizabeth and that she had finally chosen the tall, good-looking younger brother. Going on, they would say that if he had really tried, he could have easily transported his brother home quickly and safely; never mind that Simon had been badly wounded.

Such accusations would be untrue, he told himself, so why worry about them any longer. He had succeeded, and that was all that mattered. Try to think of today and all the tomorrows that will stretch ahead. I am still a young man, he mused.

During recent days and the endless nights since arriving home the life-changing experience of that journey remained constantly in his mind. He had been the one who always worried. It was he who was seldom carefree and gay but who had said that everything would work out all right. To be sure, they had finally returned home, but there was still plenty to worry about. Why could he not stop reliving that journey? Would he ever forget it?

The litter, would the straps continue to hold it together? Always watching for suitable young white oaks to cut. They certainly did wear out fast.

Oh, those kindly and sympathetic people they had met along the way. Their gifts, their heartfelt concern for Simon, their suggestions and tender care. The good Lord had watched over him and made it possible for them to meet such fine people. The weather. . . another matter. Rain, cold, wind and snow, short days and interminably long nights were what he remembered most. The road. . . there had always been that endless rut-filled road stretching out before them. Fairly good in some places, but only a muddy path through the woods in others. Rocks. Hillsides. Fallen trees. Roots. Streams. And all the while the moans and groans and incoherent mutterings of Simon. The urgency of it all. What a time he had with that brook out the other side of Springfield. And that good old man with the beard who helped him carry the litter across to the other side.

In his mind he had felt every stabbing pain and throbbing ache that Simon bore so bravely. How careful he had tried to be, caring for the brother whose pain and suffering he was only able to imagine. All the while Simon's condition worsening day by day, hour by hour. Those haunting memories. There had been tears, too. What if an accident had crippled their British horse or a sudden onrushing farm dog had caused it to spook or to run away? So many times that horse had slipped on rocks crossing streams, thrown off balance by the weight and thrust of the litter. That may have been the greatest concern. Would Simon roll off the litter and cause further damage to the wounded leg? Would he be dashed against a stone or stump?

What if there had been no doctor in the next town. The wound had needed close attention. They had said not much could be done other than keeping Simon comfortable by draining the wound, changing the dressing and otherwise trying to keep him alive. Nevertheless, it was a great comfort on those many occasions when the local doctor, hearing as most did of the arrival of an injured soldier, was able to look at Simon.

Fortunately there had been little worry over money as so many people who believed in the cause they had fought for had offered every possible aid. The all-consuming and ever present worry had been Simon's physical condition. Doctor Turner's last words seemed to still hang in his memory, "I promise nothing. Expect anything."

* * *

The scene in the door yard of Ebenezer's house at the time of their arrival was etched in Jacob's memory and would probably remain there for the rest of his life. It would have been impossible to describe his anticipation and the relief of having finally reached home with his injured brother. There were many tears as well as shouts of joy from members of the family as they had run to meet him, surrounding the British horse and the gaunt and pain-racked semiconscious man lying on the worn branches of two white oaks.

His mother's strained expression of disbelief. There was Elizabeth, the once handsome Elizabeth, her lips moving silently as she knelt tentatively on the frozen ground at her husband's side. Her thin, tear stained face was drawn by fatigue and unspeakable grief; her hair, dry and brittle from the summer's relentless sun. This image caused Jacob both pleasure and sorrow. His father stood with lowered head and in stunned silence with a look of agony and anguish on his face.

Then came Oliver, followed by the younger children. Where was Benjamin? Still on duty with Captain John Minot's Company? Ah, there, he's not home. Been in the army almost all the time since the day we all went to Concord and when he and Oliver continued right through to Cambridge. Good. Now if only Simon could be well again, and the war won as it surely will be, then we can go back to the lives we so thoroughly enjoyed before this tragic chapter.

Jacob had tried to reassure himself over and over each day that with the skill of the famous Doctor Prescott and the prayers of the family his younger brother would survive. Yet despite his own many silent prayers and his family's tireless vigil at the bedside of his comatose sibling, the outlook was dour. How could Simon ever survive? What of Doctor Oliver Prescott's somber look and the shake of his head these last few days as he looked long and hard at his gravely ill brother. Was not the famous Doctor Prescott, renowned throughout all of Middlesex County, the finest obtainable. He and that well-known dappled horse of his on whose back the doctor took occasional naps were known far and wide, working miracles on the sick. Yes, indeed no other doctor could do as well.

Ah, now for the larger logs. That back log of last night was wholly consumed. Two or three small maple logs will do for now.

But, hark! What was that muffled sound? No, no! I'm just a bit jumpy, that's all. Lately Jacob startled at sounds that a few months ago would have gone unnoticed. One of the children stirring upstairs? No. Some of the animals loose in the barn? No. It's nearer. It's clearer! Something is coming. Fast! On the road, now right in the yard!

The playing fire now lit the room, and to Jacob's horror he watched his sturdy front door out in the hall shudder under the force of a body being hurled against it. Then as strong young fists beat upon the panels, Ruthie's voice stifled by gasps and choked by fear and emotion cried out, "Jacob! Jacob! Simon's dead!

* * *

The new pastor-elect, the Reverend Daniel Chaplin closed the brief eulogy for the young soldier, Simon Patch, in the company of his grieving family and friends with the words, "Praise be to God, he is home again at last."

* * *

AFTERWARD

Simon Patch left behind his wife, Elizabeth, with four small children, one daughter and three sons. The immediate fate of Elizabeth is not known conclusively although, through the records, we do know that she remained a widow until at least February 1779.

Simon's brother, Benjamin, became guardian to the children some of whom later removed to Ludlow, Vermont. Simon's children were Rebekah, born September 11, 1770; Nathan, born December 13, 1772; Simon, born March 10, 1774 and Samuel, born July 19, 1776. Samuel was only six months old when his father died. Simon, Jr.'s marriage to Betsy Farmer in 1797 is recorded as Simon Patch "of Ludlow" in the Groton records.

Tragedy continued to haunt the Patch family after Simon's death as it was less than three weeks later when Ebenezer Patch died on January 19, 1777. Whether his death was hastened by grief cannot be known. Death had previously been no stranger to Ebenezer's family He and Sarah had lost several young children, most likely due to infectious disease. Before this story begins, in 1763 three-year-old Samuel died on May 20th of that year. Two years later Ebenezer Jr. died on July 9, 1765, at four years of age. In 1770 little daughter Sarah died on April 2nd at age thirteen, and another daughter, Sarah, named for the first Sarah, died in 1771. All of these children are buried in the Old Burying Ground, in Groton, Massachusetts.

The loss of Simon, however, must have been bittersweet. Adult children are not supposed to die before their parents, so it is instinctively believed; and Simon's death must have been particularly painful to Ebenezer, apparently not in good health himself.

Ebenezer's widow, Sarah Wright, did not remarry for several years. In November 1784 she married Samuel Chamberlain of Hollis, and she lived for another nine years, dying June 12, 1793, at the age of sixty three. Her epitaph in the Old Burying Ground reads, "Here lies the body of Mrs. Sarah Chamberlain wife of Samuel Chamberlain and late wife of Mr. Ebenezer Patch who died June ye 12, 1793 in the 64th year of her age." She is listed as a Patriot in the Daughters of the American Revolution records, a distinction awarded for her contribution to the cause of clothing.

Jacob had been married for only about three years when this story begins. He later became a Corporal in the Continental Army and lived until December 22, 1818, when he was run over by a horse. His grave in the Old Burying Ground is marked by a Revolutionary War flag. His wife, Mary, was the daughter of Benjamin Hazen and Bette Nutting. Mary lived to be 85 years of age, out-living Jacob by ten years. They had several children: Jacob, born November 22, 1772, became a doctor and died in Camden, Maine, in 1846; Sarah and Jesse both died young; Mary, born March 27, 1778, married Josiah Spaulding; David, born January 11, 1780, married Sally Heald of Westford and removed apparently to Wallingford, Vermont; Lydia, born January 24, 1782, married Ephram Heald, Jr.; Zara, born January 21, 1784, married first Susanna Nutting, then Hannah Nutting and finally Mrs. Emily E. Fitch; and Edmund, born February 24, 1786, married Philomela Lawrence of Groton

Benjamin and his wife, Persis Lewis, were admitted to the church in Groton, Massachusetts, on December 9, 1781, and dismissed to the church in Ludlow, Vermont, on September 8, 1793. They were among the early settlers of Ludlow. Benjamin also became a Corporal. He lived until 1827 and died on September 28th in Ludlow where he is buried with his wife and several children. In addition to marching on the Alarm of April 19, 1775, he was paid for mileage to and from Dorchester Heights, eighty two miles and two days travel, warrant allowed in Concord November 30, 1776.

He also served in Lieutenant John Flint's Company, Colonel Thomas Poor's Regiment, enlisting June 17, 1778, and discharged February 11, 1779, for service of eight months, seven days at and about White Plains including eleven days travel home (220 miles). His regiment was raised to fortify the passes of North River, New York. During June through August of that year his service was dated Fort Clinton. He was on the payroll for September 1778 dated West Point and payroll for November 1778 also for West Point. Regrettably for many years his service to this country was not recognized by a Revolutionary grave marker.

In addition to raising Simon's children, Benjamin and his wife had the following children of their own: Persis, born 1781, married Dr. William A. Wetherbee; Emma, baptized in 1783, married Deacon John Davison; Sarah, baptized 1786, married Elias Sergeant; Benjamin, Jr., born 1788; Roswell, born 1791; Jonathan, born 1793; Ezra, born 1795, died at age 16; Truman, born 1798; Alden, born 1800, married Sally Spaulding of Cavendish; and perhaps others.

Ebenezer Patch's young son Oliver is not a major character in this story, yet his service to this country is noteworthy. He served as a Corporal in Captain Asa Lawrence's Company of Minutemen that marched on the alarm of April 19, 1775, to the headquarters in Cambridge; his service was six days. He enlisted April 25, 1775, in the Army and served as Sergeant in Captain Asa Lawrence's Company, Colonel William Prescott's Regiment, muster roll dated August 1, 1775, service ninety eight days. Company return dated

October 6, 1775. He was wounded in his right shoulder in the Battle of Bunker Hill.

Oliver did not marry until 1778 when he took as his bride Alethea Blood, and they removed from Groton after 1790 to an unknown location. Alethea's brother, Abraham, was killed at Bunker Hill on June 17, 1775. Oliver and Alethea had several children: Oliver, William, Reuben, Henry, Luther and Nahum.

Young Ruthie grew up and married on December 7, 1780, Elnathan Sawtell who attained the rank of Lieutenant in the Army, participating in the Revolution. They inherited the Patch homestead and eventually removed to Littleton. Ruth died on December 16, 1831, at sixty eight years of age, and Lieutenant Elnathan Sawtell died August 31,1836, at eighty three years of age. They both rest in Groton's Old Burying Ground.

Little Ede, married Israel Shattuck in Pepperell, Massachusetts, on May 28, 1789. After Ebenezer died, Amos Ames became guardian to both Ruthie and Ede.

Hinchman Warren of Townsend married Esther Taylor on Feb. 1, 1781. Their graves are located in the Pleasant View Cemetery in Mason, New Hampshire. Hinch died May 4, 1827, at seventy five years of age, and Esther died December 21, 1843, at eighty eight years of age. An infant child rests beside them. Their son Jonathan was born Mar. 25, 1782, and their daughter Lydia was born Sept. 26, 1783.

John and Samuel Gragg were sick and sent home from White Plains. Both participated in later campaigns. Benjamin Fisk saw no further service.

* * *

Today Ashby, Massachusetts, is a small, rural town nestled in the northern part of the state near the New Hampshire border. A designated historic district, it contains churches along with town buildings and a few residential homes. Its small-town character has been retained through the many years since the first settlers chose to plant their roots down into its soil. Home to fewer than 900 families, it is crime-free, bucolic and reminiscent of days gone by with its rolling viridian hills, fragrant, colorful orchards and small hay farms. Miles of blue-gray stone walls abound, creating the pastoral appearance of yesteryear. There is no longer any industry in Ashby. Most working folks commute to out-of-town jobs, yet a few small businesses support those individuals lucky enough to be able to work from home. Urban sprawl has not yet come to Ashby. Perhaps it never will. Only time will tell.

The town's first settlers arrived in 1676 when it was home to only forty three families, and it was nearly a century later before incorporation occurred just a few years before the outbreak of the Revolutionary War. That was nearly 250 years ago. Many families have come and gone since then, and many desperate lives have been spent, nurturing the same soil that covers the town's terrain today.

* * *

For more than 300 years and all throughout the history of America many, many families have sacrificed their sons and daughters to win and to preserve the freedoms we enjoy today. Fathers, mothers, wives and sweethearts have shed untold tears and spent countless sleepless nights worrying about the welfare of those on the battle-field. Few families have served their country more nobly or sacri-ficed more than the family of Patch as described in this story.

Some might say that some of the "battles" fought during the Revolution were not really battles at all but merely skirmishes at best; but to the people who participated in them and who lived through those harrowing times, they represented periods of extreme sacrifice, anxiety and sometimes of terror. Compare, if you will, the lives we live today with the lives of the Patch family members for example and remember, if you will, that had it not been for the folks of that day, we would not live as we do now.

This was not a family of great wealth or learning. They were simple people, very ordinary, in fact. Tangible possessions were passed from one generation to the next as was the practice at the time. Land was acquired as opportunities and personal resources became available, but the Patches, unlike many of their peers were not land speculators. As each surviving child inherited from the estates of his or her parents, farms were broken up into smaller and smaller pieces making them eventually uneconomic.

Who knows why some of the Patch boys left Groton. Perhaps the memories were too painful to bear. Perhaps they sought economic opportunity for themselves as well as for their children elsewhere. Perhaps it was a stirring wanderlust that led them off into the frontier. Why did Jacob, Jr. become a doctor?

We leave these unanswered questions to the imagination of the reader and hope that in the telling of this story we leave the reader with a deeper appreciation for the blessings and opportunities this country offers as well as a brief glimpse into the lives of this 18th century American family.

✳ ✳ ✳

BIBLIOGRAPHY
AND NOTES

Bates, Issachar. "The Revolutionary War and Issachar Bates". Old Chatham, New York. The Chatham Courier Company. 1960.

Bell, John. Discourse on the Nature and Care of Wounds. Volume I. Walpole, New Hampshire. Printed for Thomas and Justin Hinds. 1807.

_____. "Notebook of Reverend Jeremy Belnap". Proceedings XIV.93, Massachusetts Historical Society. June 1875.

Brooks, Noah. Henry Knox–Soldier of the Revolution. Putnam Books. 1900.

Butler, Caleb. History of the Town of Groton. Boston. Press of T. R. Marvin. 1848.

Callahan, North. Henry Knox–General Washington's General. New York. Rinehart. 1958.

Coffin, Charles Carleton. The Boys of '76. New York. Harper & Brothers Publishers. 1876.

_____. "1816 Controversy on Christmas", Historical Society Publication

Cooper, Samuel. <u>Practice of Surgery.</u> Hanover. Justin Hines Publisher. 1815.

Crawford, Mary Caroline. <u>Among Old New England Inns.</u> Boston. L. C. Page & Company. 1907.

Dorland, William. <u>American Illustrated Medical Dictionary.</u> W. B. Saunders Co. 1906.

Drake, Samuel Adams. <u>History of Middlesex County,</u> "Ashby", Volume I. Boston. Estes and Lauriat Publishers. 1880. pp. 217-225.

Duncan, Louis C. <u>Medical Men in the American Revolution 1775-1783.</u> Carlisle Barracks, Pennsylvania. Medical Field Service School.

Earle, Alice Morse. <u>Stage Coach and Tavern Days</u>. Boston. MacMillan Company.

Essex Institute. <u>Essex Institute Historical Collection.</u> Salem, Massachusetts. Essex Institute Press. 1859.

Greene, Samuel A., M.D. <u>Epitaphs from the Old Burying Ground in Groton,</u>

<u>Massachusetts.</u> Boston. Little, Brown and Company. 1878.

Greene, Samuel A., M.D. <u>An Historical Sketch of Groton, Massachusetts 1655-1890.</u>

Reprinted from The History of Middlesex County, Massachusetts. Edited by D. H. Hurd. 1890. Greene, Samuel A., M.D. et. al. Three Military Diaries Kept by Groton Soldiers. J. Wilson. 1901.

Greene, Samuel A., M.D. "Groton during the Revolution". History of Chelmsford Massachusetts. 1917.

Greene, Samuel A., M.D. Greene's Historical Series, II.

Hill, John B. Old Dunstable (April 19, 1775). Nashua, New Hampshire. E. H. Spaulding. 1878.

Hill, John B. "Battle of Bunker Hill as told by John B. Hill, a grandson of Colonel Ebenezer Bancroft.

_____. History of Westchester County, Volume I. Chicago. Lewis Publishing Company. 1899.

_____. "History of Livestock Raising in the United States 1607-1806". Wyoming. American Heritage Center. Box 62. Folder 9. 1942.

Hopeland, Otto. Westchester County during the American Revolution 1775-1783. White Plains, New York. Westchester County Historical Society, Volume III.

Jenkins, Stephen. Old Boston Post Road. New York. G. P. Putnam and Sons. 1913.

Jones, John. <u>Plain Concise Practical Remarks for the Treatment of Wounds and Fractures.</u> Philadelphia. Robert T. Bell Publishers. 1776.

_____. "The Lexington-Concord Battle Road". Concord, Massachusetts. Chamber of Commerce.

Love, William Deloss, Jr. <u>Fast and Thanksgiving Days of New England.</u> Boston. Houghton, Mifflin & Co. 1895.

_____. "Magazine of American History". Volume 28. New York. MacMillan and Co.pp. 241-256.

Marlowe, George Francis. <u>Coaching Roads of Old New England.</u> New York. MacMillan and Co. 1945.

Mead, David M. <u>History of Greenwich.</u> New York. 1857.

Mead, Spencer P., LLB. <u>Ye Historic of Ye Town of Greenwich.</u> 1911.

Mitchell, Isabel S. <u>Roads and Road Making in Colonial Connecticut.</u> New Haven. Yale University Press. 1933.

_____. <u>Prescott Memorial 1870, Part I.</u> Reprinted by Ward Publishing Co. 1983.

_____. Records of Middlesex South District Registry of Deeds, Commonwealth of Massachusetts, book 79, p. 408-410.

Roca-Garcia, Helen. "Bayberry Candles." Horticulture, September 1962, p. 441.

Scharf, Thomas. <u>History of Westchester County, Volume II.</u> New York. Preston & Company. 1886. p. 277.

Stiles, Henry R. <u>The History of Ancient Wetherfield, Connecticut.</u> New York. 1904.

Stuart, I. W. <u>Life of Captain Nathan Hale—Martyr Spy of the Revolution.</u> Hartford, Connecticut. F. A. Brown. 1856.

Temple, Josiah Howard. <u>History of Palmer, Massachusetts.</u> Town of Palmer. 1889.

Tilton, James, M.D. <u>Economic Observations on Military Hospitals—and the Prevention and Cure of Diseases Incident to an Army.</u> Delaware. J. Wilson. 1813.

Varney, George Jones. <u>The Story of Patriot's Day, Concord and Lexington, April 19, 1775.</u> Boston. Lee and Shepard Publishers. 1895.

Ward, Elizabeth. <u>Old Times in Shrewsbury.</u> New York. McGeorge Printing Company. 1892.

Wells, Jesse D. "Nathan Hale". Manchester Union Leader. February 22, 1962.

Wheeldon, William W. <u>Men at the North Bridge, April 19, 1775.</u> Boston. Lee & Shepard Publishers, No 10 Milk Street. 1885.

Wheeldon, William W. <u>New Chapter in the History of Concord Fight, Groton Minute Men at the North Bridge, April 19, 1775.</u>

Wood, Frederick J. <u>Turnpikes of New England</u>. Boston. Marshall Jones Company. 1919.

Wright, H. W. <u>Route of Colonel Knox through Western Massachusetts.</u> Springfield, Massachusetts. 1925.

_____. "Prudence Wright and the Women who guarded the Bridge, Pepperell, Massachusetts, April 1775." Historical Society Papers. (Prudence was the daughter of Samuel Cummings and descended from John Lawrence of Groton. She was born November 26, 1740 in the Parish of West Dunstable, later Hollis. She and David Wright were married December 8, 1761. She was 35 years old when this event occurred.)

Made in the USA
Middletown, DE
22 December 2014